How To...

Improvise Over Chord Changes

By Shawn Wallace, Dr. Keith Newton, Kris Johnson & Steve Kortyka

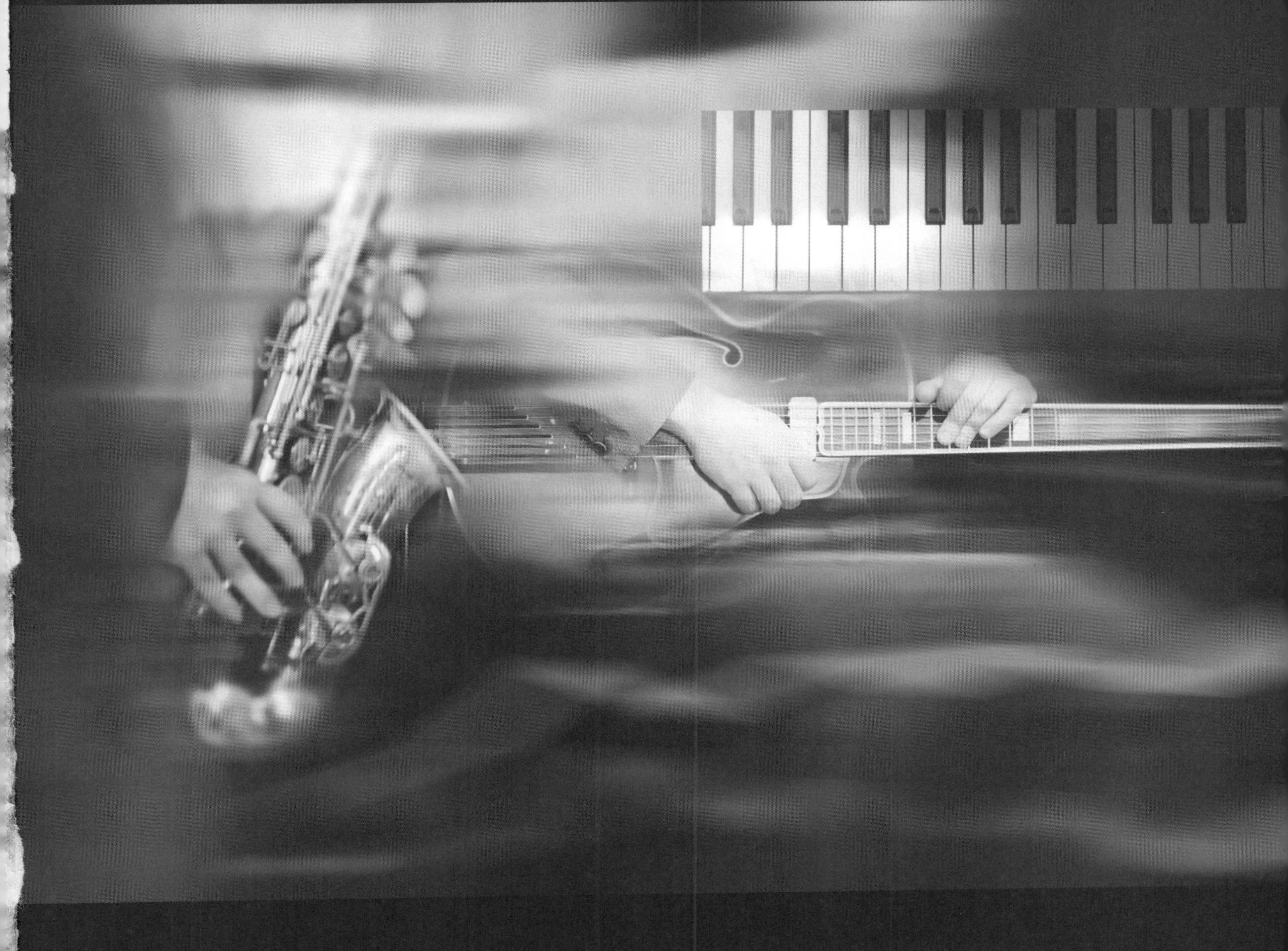

ISBN 978-1-4950-0192-5

Visit Hal Leonard Online at
www.halleonard.com

Contact Us:
Hal Leonard
7777 West Bluemound Road
Milwaukee, WI 53213
Email: info@halleonard.com

In Europe contact:
Hal Leonard Europe Limited
Distribution Centre, Newmarket Road
Bury St Edmunds, Suffolk, IP33 3YB
Email: info@halleonardeurope.com

In Australia contact:
Hal Leonard Australia Pty. Ltd.
4 Lentara Court
Cheltenham, Victoria, 3192 Australia
Email: info@halleonard.com.au

CONTENTS

INTRODUCTION

This book is step-by-step guide to help students develop essential skills for improvisation. The concepts presented will first be demonstrated over the blues progression; in later chapters, the concepts will be realized over rhythm changes and in original compositions based on the chord progressions of challenging jazz standards.

The information herein has been compiled primarily from material presented in my improvisation classes, as well as in my applied lesson studio, at The Ohio State University. The development of the book, however, occurred through collaboration between colleagues. While teaching improvisational concepts in my courses at OSU, I teamed up with Dr. Keith Newton (then a graduate student) and Steve Kortyka (also then a graduate student, now touring and working with Lady Gaga and Tony Bennett, with whom he won a Grammy). Kris Johnson, then working at The Ohio State University as the Jazz Trumpet Instructor and Jazz Arranging/Composition teacher, was also approached to join the group. I couldn't have completed the task without the countless hours of tedious work each of these fine gentlemen contributed. They helped define improvisational concepts through exercises and created invaluable content that has solidified the systematic layout of this book. I hold deep admiration for each of them and have been tremendously blessed and touched by their commitment, dedication, focus, and support.

Each concept is presented in an organized and progressive format; it may be utilized by improvisers of all ability levels. Though not primarily based upon technical studies, regular practice of the exercises will greatly improve technical facility. Technique is involved in every communication. Improvisation is no different. If you are fluent in F major but not fluent in F♯ major, then improvisation in F♯ major will be more limited than in F major. Spontaneity requires preparation. To that end, this book is full of exercises with the express intent of equipping you with the tools for improvisation.

Writing this text has been an immense journey; in the creation of materials, we found ourselves constantly in dialogue, working to more clearly define terms that have been long-standing, but not utilized consistently, within jazz pedagogy. Standardization in jazz pedagogy is not likely to occur anytime soon; however, a concerted effort has been made to apply terminology uniformly across the text. In the application of concepts, similar efforts have been made to formalize and standardize the language used.

We believe you will find *How to Improvise Over Chord Changes* an excellent means of continuing your journey along the continuum of musicianship – be you beginner, amateur, professional, or pedagogue.

– Shawn "Thunder" Wallace

CHAPTER 1

PRIMER

Concepts, Scales, and Modes

- Chord Scale Theory
- Tertian Harmony
- Basic Chords and Extended Harmony

In this chapter, you will be introduced to the basic concepts and terminology needed for a foundational study of blues and jazz harmony. You will learn the fundamental vocabulary of chord-scale theory and explore the harmonic structures necessary for the application of chord scales. Do not move on to new concepts until your understanding of the term or the music theory is firmly entrenched in your brain. You can do it!

CHORD-SCALE THEORY

Chord-scale theory refers to the practice of applying particular scales to chord progressions as the basis of improvisation. Chord-scale theories are based on the principle that every chord has a scale, in most cases diatonic to itself, that can be exploited to create melodies using notes applicable to that chord. Simply put, every chord represents a simultaneous sounding of intervallic notes within a scale; every scale is a representation of a chord. This association between chords and scales is sometimes called chord-scale.

Chord-scales can help improvisers increase fluency and augment harmonic and melodic capabilities. Chord-scales may be applied linearly, intervallically, or in any manner applicable to the appropriate harmonic context. To become a competent improviser, you'll need a thorough knowledge of chord-scales.

Chord-Scale Basics

1. Every chord has a corresponding scale.
2. Every scale has a corresponding chord.

Chord-Scale Basic Example

A chord-scale contains only notes that are diatonic (within the chord or key center) to the chord presented. The application of chord-scales provides an improviser with theoretical practice to create melodies diatonic to a chord (or chord progression); it also furnishes material that may not be evident through other means – such as improvising by ear without a knowledge of chord-scales.

Chord-scale theory is best used as a training tool

Great improvisation is dependent not only on knowledgeable application of chord-scales, but also on technical facility and musicianship developed through performance and listening experience. As jazz trombonist and educator Hal Crook has stated, the pioneers of jazz improvisation relied on their "listening/hearing skills and their ability to accurately outline basic chord sound to guide their improvising and to create inspired melodies." To that end, chord-scales can be used to supplement your innate ability to spontaneously hear and respond to musical stimuli.

TERMS AND CONCEPTS

Diatonic: Notes within the key, chord, or tonal center.

Passing tones: Notes outside the key, chord, or tonal center.

Tertian harmony: Chords built in 3rds. Tertian harmony includes triads, 7th chords, and extended harmony (9ths, 11ths, and 13ths).

Chord: Two or more notes sounding simultaneously. In this text, chords usually refer to three or more notes sounding simultaneously.

Chord progression: A series of chords played in succession. Chord progressions help establish key and tonal centers within an entire musical work or within a section of a musical work.

Scale: Any set of musical notes organized by fundamental frequency or pitch. A scale may be organized by ascending pitch or by descending pitch.

Interval: Refers to the harmonic distance between two pitches. The pitches may be sounded sequentially or simultaneously (as in a chords).

ABOUT TERTIAN HARMONY

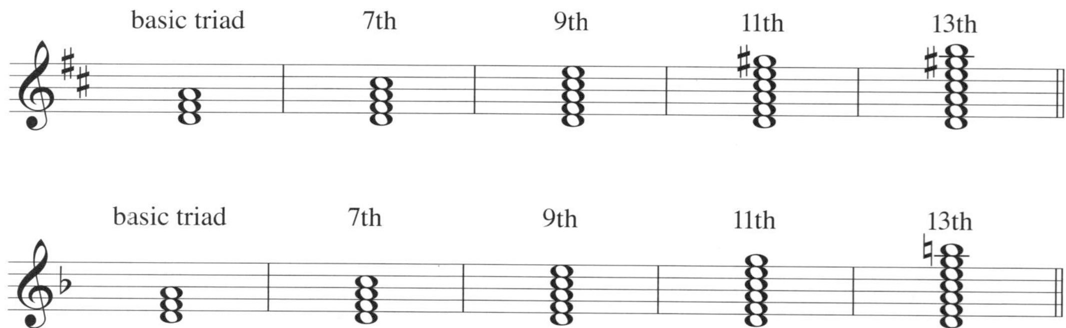

Tertian harmony is the primary harmonic system for Western music; it is employed extensively in chord-scale theory. This system of harmony features chords constructed vertically in 3rds, as shown in the chart above. Let's see how this works.

TRIADS

Triads are three-note chords. Like other chords in tertian harmony, triads are constructed in 3rds. There are four basic types: major, minor, augmented, and diminished. These are shown below in root position.

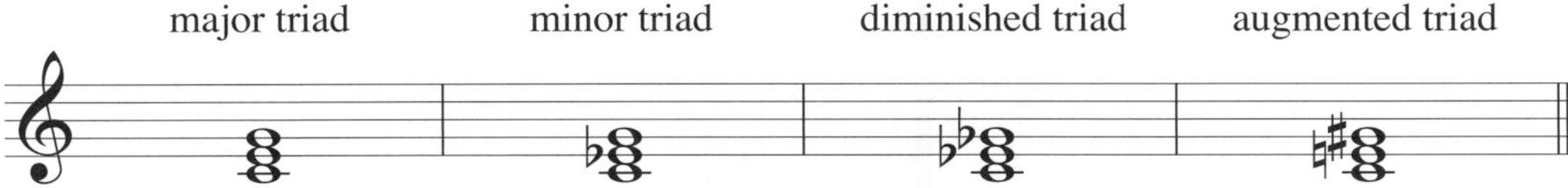

Major Triads

Major triads are constructed using one major 3rd (M3) and one minor 3rd (m3) stacked vertically; for example, a root-position C major triad = C-E-G, a major 3rd (C-E) plus a minor 3rd (E-G).

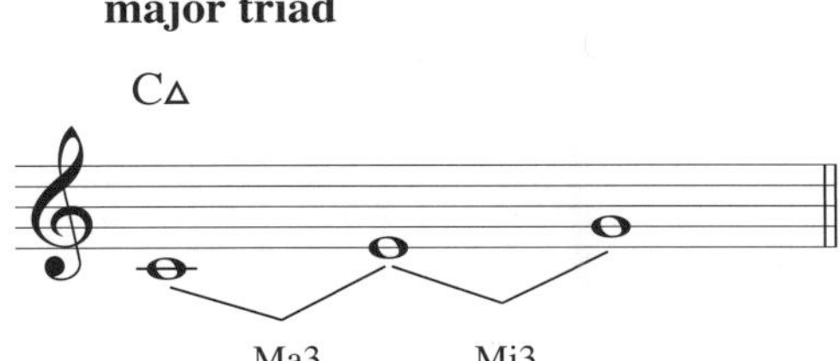

Minor Triads

Minor triads are constructed using one minor 3rd (m3) and one major 3rd (M3) stacked vertically; for example, a root-position C minor triad = C-E♭-G, a minor 3rd (C-E♭) plus a major 3rd (E♭-G).

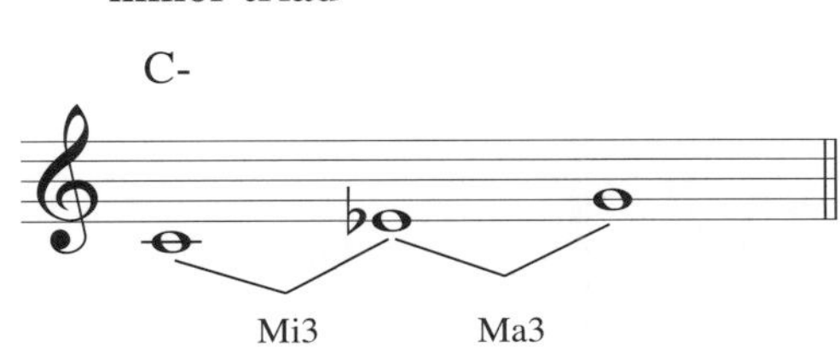

Augmented Triads

Augmented triads are constructed using two major 3rds (M3) stacked vertically; for example, a C augmented triad = C-E-G♯, a major 3rd (C-E) plus a major 3rd (E-G♯).

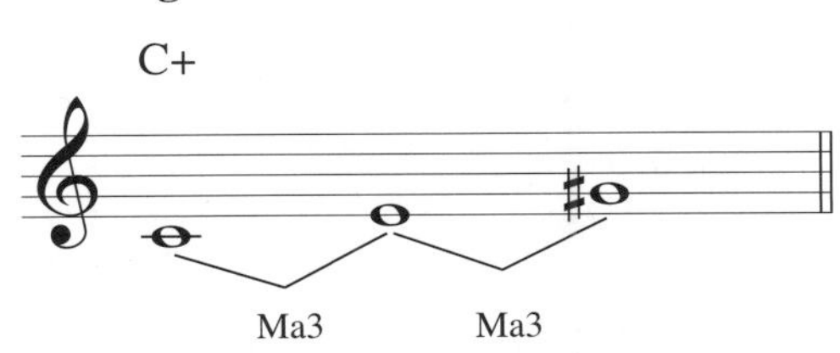

Diminished Triads

Diminished triads are constructed using two minor 3rds (m3) stacked vertically; for example, a C diminished triad = C-E♭-G♭, a minor 3rd (C-E♭) plus a minor 3rd (E♭-G♭).

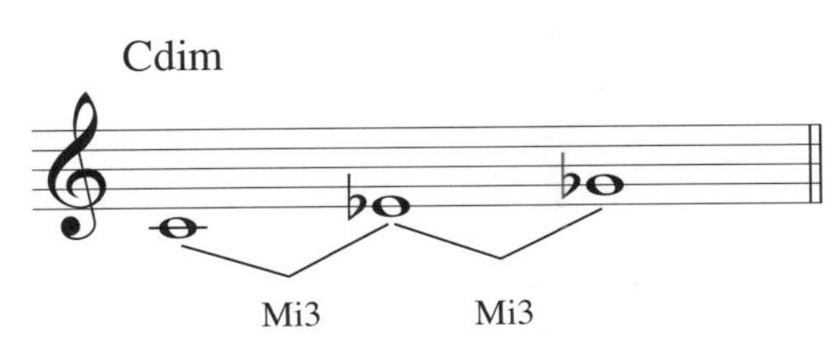

SEVENTH (7th) CHORDS

Seventh (7th) chords are four-note chords. In tertian harmony, 7th chords have an additional major 3rd (M3) or minor 3rd (m3) superimposed over the triad. The following are examples of the most common 7th chords:

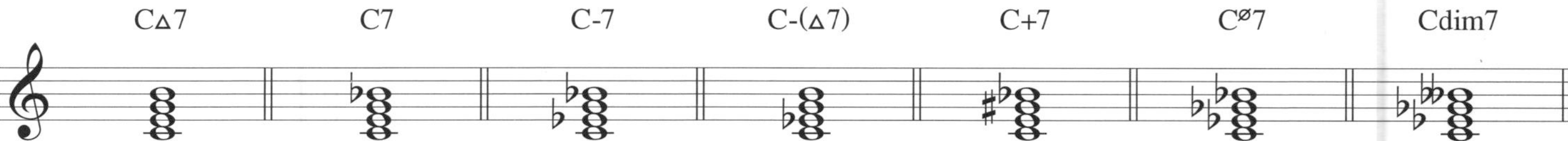

Major 7th Chord

A major 7th chord consists of a major triad plus a major 3rd (M3); for example, Cmaj7 = C-E-G-B, a C major triad (C-E-G) plus a major 3rd (G-B).

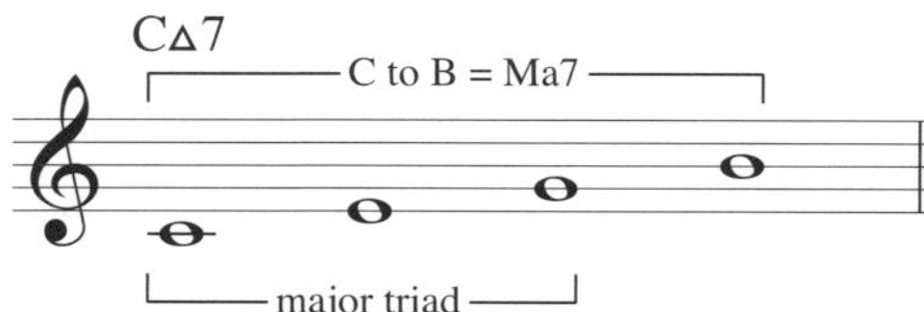

Dominant 7th Chord

A dominant 7th chord consists of a major triad plus a minor 3rd (m3); for example, C7 = C-E-G-B♭, a C major triad (C-E-G) plus a minor 3rd (G-B♭).

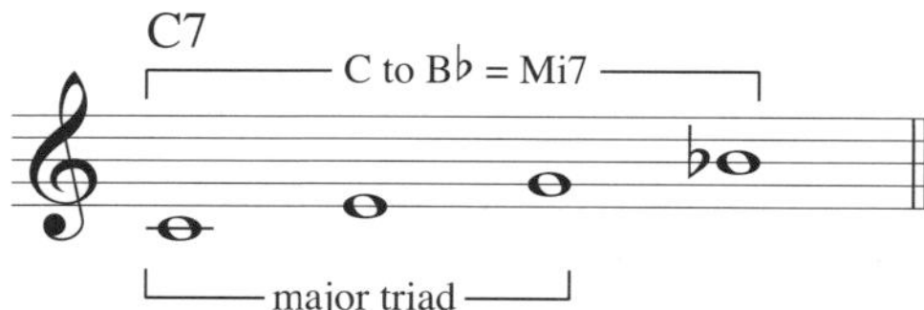

Minor 7th Chord

A minor 7th chord consists of a minor triad plus a minor 3rd (m3); for example, Cm7 = C-E♭-G-B♭, a C minor triad (C-E♭-G) plus a minor 3rd (G-B♭).

Minor-Major 7th Chord

A minor-major 7th chord consists of a minor triad plus a major 3rd; for example, Cm(maj7) = C-E♭-G-B, a C major triad (C-E♭-G) plus a major 3rd (G-B).

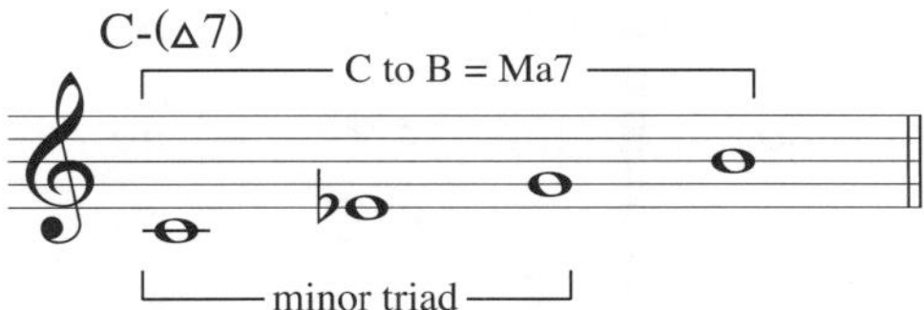

Augmented 7th Chord

An augmented 7th chord consists of an augmented triad plus a minor 3rd; for example, C+7 (Cmaj7♯5) = C-E-G♯-B, a C augmented triad (C-E-G♯) plus a minor 3rd (G♯-B)

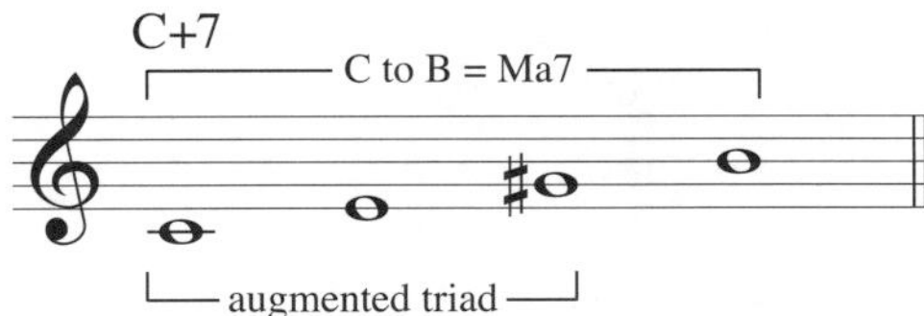

Half-Diminished 7th Chord

A half-diminished 7th chord consists of a diminished triad plus a major 3rd; for example, Cø7 (Cm7♭5) = C-E♭-G♭-B♭, a C diminished triad (C-E♭-G♭) plus a major 3rd (G♭-B♭).

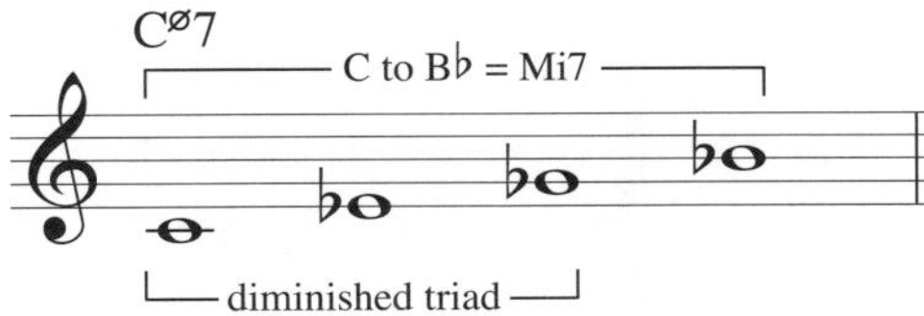

Fully Diminished 7th Chord

A fully diminished 7th chord consists of a diminished triad plus a minor 3rd; for example, C°7 = C-E♭-G♭-B𝄫, a C diminished triad (C-E♭-G♭) plus a minor 3rd (G♭-B𝄫).

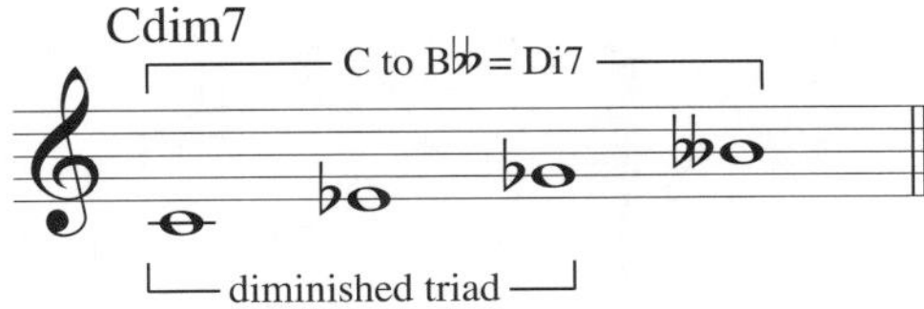

TERTIAN HARMONY:
EXTENDED CHORD HARMONIES (9ths, 11ths, 13ths)

Extended chords superimpose additional major 3rds (M3) or minor 3rds (m3) onto existing 7th chords. The harmonies may extend vertically until notes that already exist in the chord reappear.

The following are common examples of extended chord harmonies:

Extended Chord Harmonies, Example #1

Major

C6 | C6/9 | (D∆/C∆) C6/9(♯11)

C∆7 | C∆9 | C∆9♯11 | (D∆/C∆) C∆13♯11

Dominant

C7 | C9 | C9♯11 | C13♯11

Altered Dominant

C7♭9 | C7♯11(♭9) | (D♯dim/C7) C13♯11(♭9) | C7♭13(♯11,♭9)

C7♯9 | C7♯11(♯9) | (D♯dim/C7) C13♯11(♯9) | C7♭13(♯11,♯9)

C+7 | C9♯5 | C9♯11(♯5) | (D∆/C7♯5) C13♯11(♯5)

C7♭9(♯5) | C7♯11(♭9,♯5) | (F♯-/C7♯5) C13♯11(♯9,♯5)

C7♯9(♯5) | C7♯11(♯9,♯5) | (D♯dim/C7♯5) C13♯11(♯9,♯5)

Extended Chord Harmonies Example #2

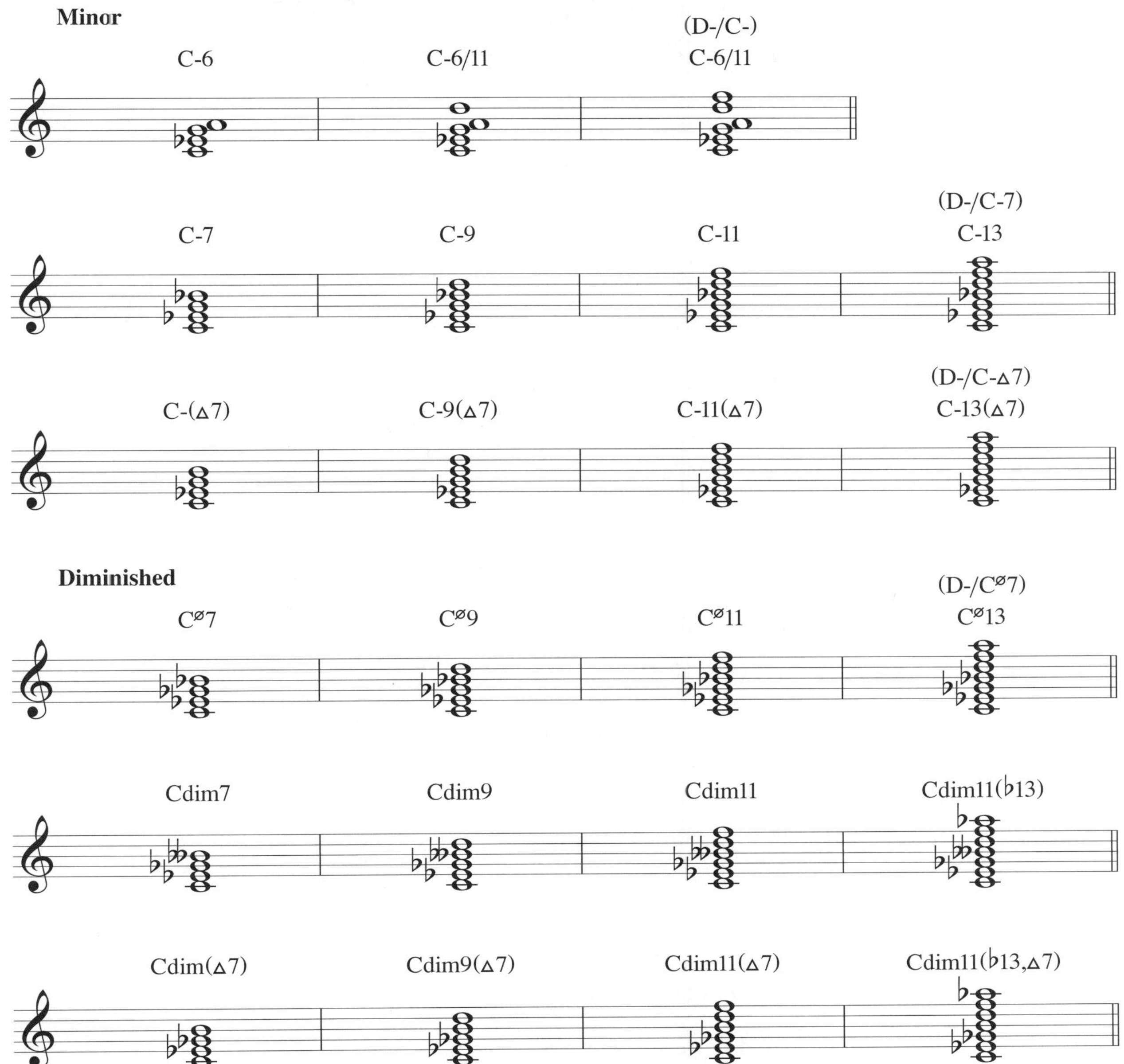

CHAPTER 2

RIFF-BASED IMPROVISATION – BLUES & RHYTHM CHANGES

Concepts, Scales, and Modes

- Kansas City Scale
- Blues Scale
- Riff Harmony

In this chapter, you will identify simple riffs and chord changes for later use in improvisation for blues and rhythm changes. Regular repetition of these exercises will begin the process of augmenting your ability to hear, relate to the chords and scales, and recognize basic melodic forms. Practice these exercises and become familiar with each musical concept. You can do it!

A *riff* is defined as a "short, rhythmic, melodic phrase that is often repeated." In our studies, we'll look at three different types of riffs.

- riffs that target the key center
- riffs that outline the voice leading
- riffs that outline the chord quality

This guide will provide several techniques for improvising using riffs. While many riffs can be based on certain scales and chords, listening to classic recordings that show its depth is the best way to develop an understanding of this concept. The techniques explored here are based upon the substantive study of blues riffs found on recordings and in the melodies, shout choruses, and background figures used in the jazz canon.

Learning these riffs by ear will strengthen aural skills, expand technique, focus sound, and – most importantly – teach you how to swing and match phrasing. It will also keep you from getting locked into one concept, instead using all the techniques you learn to form fluency in this musical language.

Here are a few recordings that demonstrate some of the concepts:

- *The Swinger* Harry "Sweets" Edison
- *Back to Back* Duke Ellington and Johnny Hodges
- *Ben and Sweets* Ben Webster and Harry "Sweets" Edison
- *Live at the Sands* Count Basie Orchestra

Let's begin by looking at the blues form and discussing two scales commonly used to create riff-based melodies.

KANSAS CITY SCALE

The Kansas City Scale uses the 1, 2, ♭3, 5, and 6 degrees of the major scale. It has the same structure as major pentatonic scale (a five-note scale created using scale degrees 1, 2, 3, 5, and 6 of a major scale, see page 23), but with a lowered 3rd.

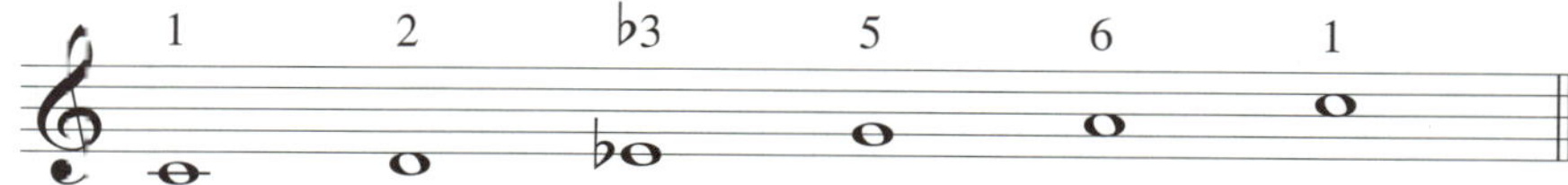

Here are three famous examples of blues riffs that use the Kansas City Scale. These have been transposed to the key of C.

BLUES SCALE

The blues scale uses scale degrees 1, ♭3, 4, ♭5, 5, and ♭7 of the major scale. The format of this can also be thought of as a minor pentatonic scale (a five-note scale created using the 1st, ♭3rd, 4th, 5th, and ♭7th scale degrees when compared to a major scale), with an added ♭5th (or ♯4th).

12-BAR BLUES

In this section, we'll think of the blues in three phrases. Each phrase is four bars in length. Although blues riffs typically use call-and-response within a four-bar phrase, the blues form can also be outlined repeating a single four-bar phrase three times. The following example shows a 12-bar blues in C, with riffs that use the blues scale. Practice playing these phrases. On page 15, we'll get into the specifics of the blues progression.

RIFF HARMONY

Often, a riff that uses either scale can have an easy harmony added to it by using the interval of a minor 3rd (m3). A Kansas City Scale transposed up a minor 3rd (m3), for example, uses the same notes of the blues scale without the natural 5th:

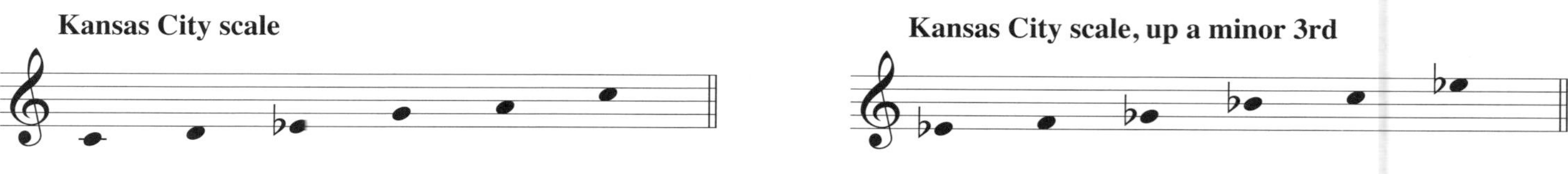

Alternatively, a blues scale transposed down a minor 3rd (m3) will feel like the Kansas City Scale with an added major 3rd:

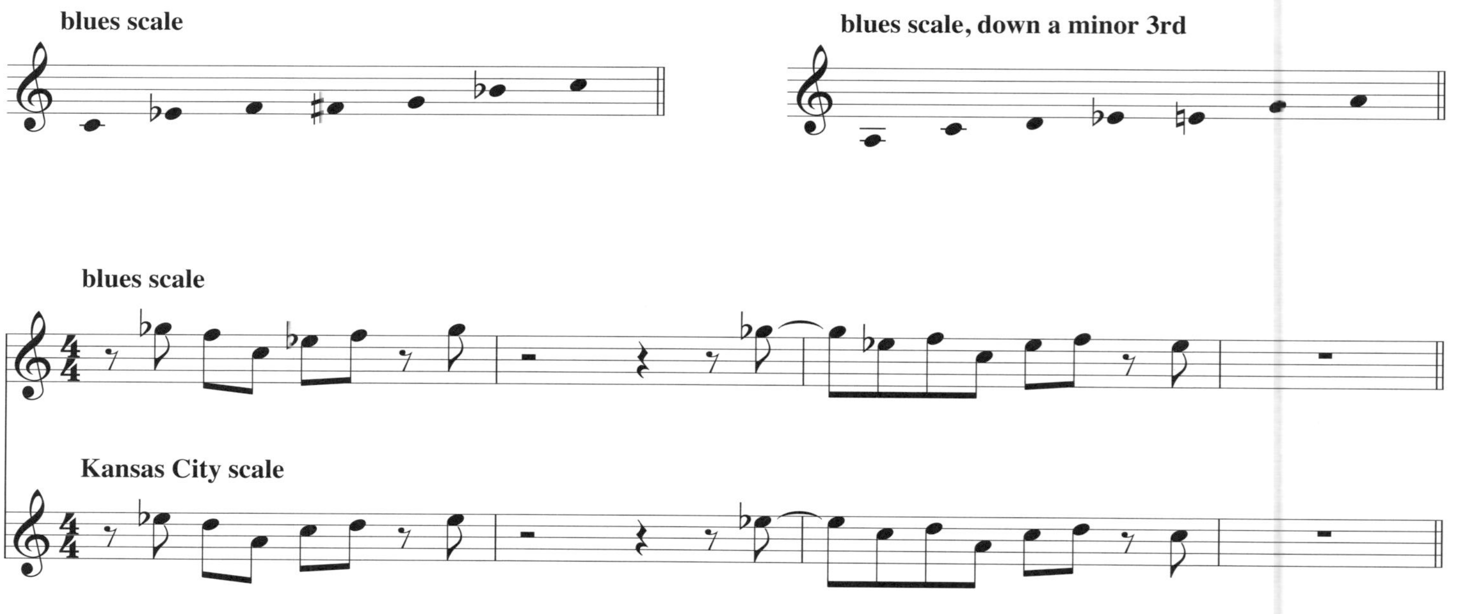

Note that when the ♮5th of the blues scale is used, the harmony utilizes a major 3rd (M3).

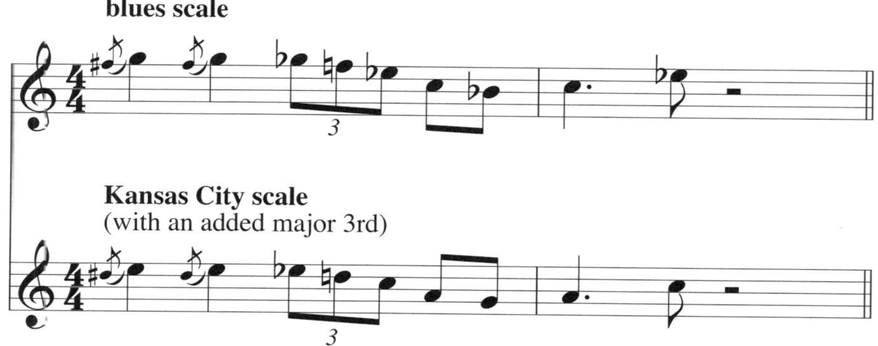

BLUES PROGRESSION

There are many variations on the 12-bar blues progression. In this example, a progression in C major that uses dominant chords based on I, IV, and V is shown.

- **tonic (I):** the home key of the blues
- **subdominant (IV):** the chord four scale degrees above the tonic chord
- **dominant (V):** the chord five scale degrees above the tonic chord

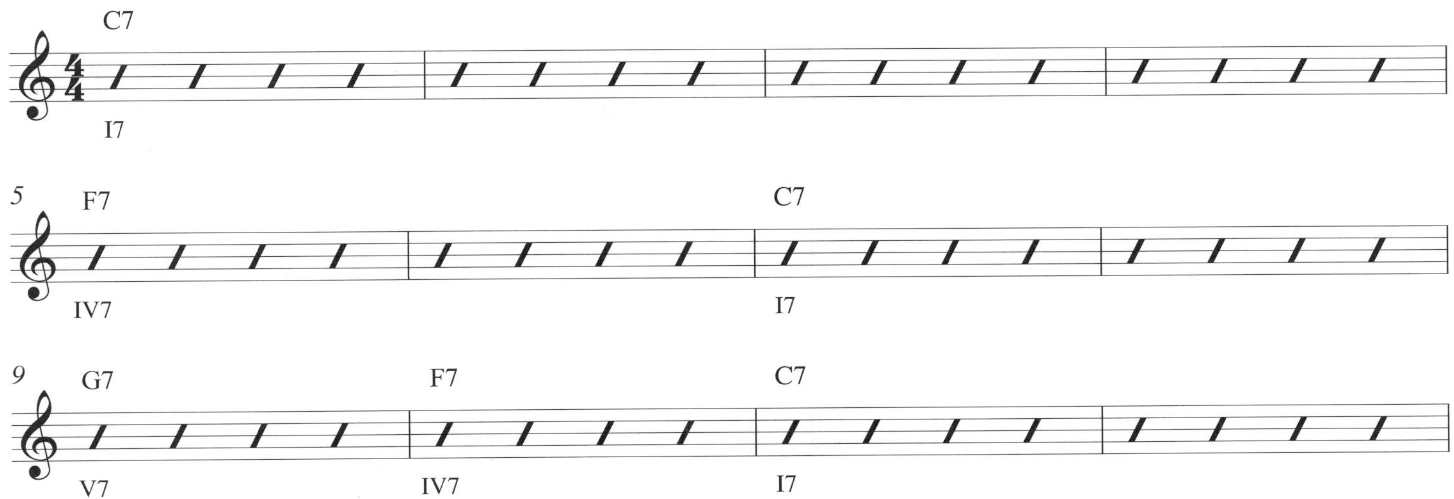

Explore this blues progression further by arpeggiating each of the chords on beats 1 and 2, as shown below.

DOMINANT RIFFS

Like the blues scale and Kansas City Scale, riffs can be created using the notes of the dominant chord. Here are two examples based on C7.

The following three riffs are in C, but can be transposed into F and G and played in time over the form.

Example 1

Example 2

It is also common to add passing tones and approaching tones within the dominant sound.

Example 3

II–V–I TURNAROUND

A common variation to the blues form adds the IV chord in the second bar. Another common variation replaces the V–IV progression used in bars 9 and 10 with a II–V–I progression. Sometimes both the II and V will be dominant (II7 and V7), and often the II will be minor 7th (ii7) and the V dominant (V7). When using chord riffs, an effective way to capture this sound is to use both II7 and V7.

C7
F7
C7
5
F7
C7
9
D7
G7
C7
II7
V7
I7

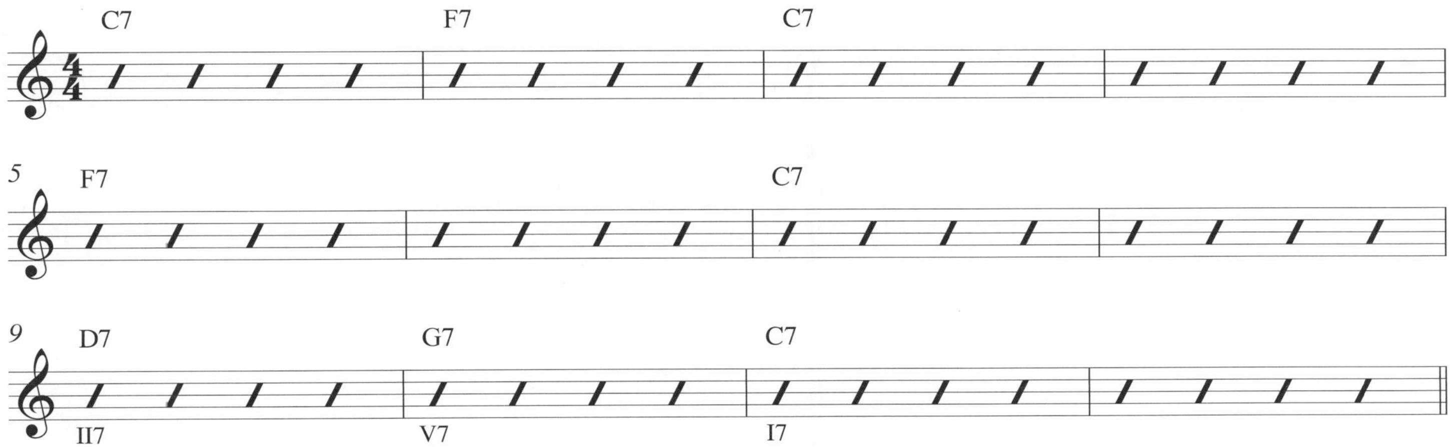

The following three examples utilize several of our chord riffs, applied to variations on the blues form. Add these to your improvising vocabulary; practice until they feel like second nature to you.

Example 1

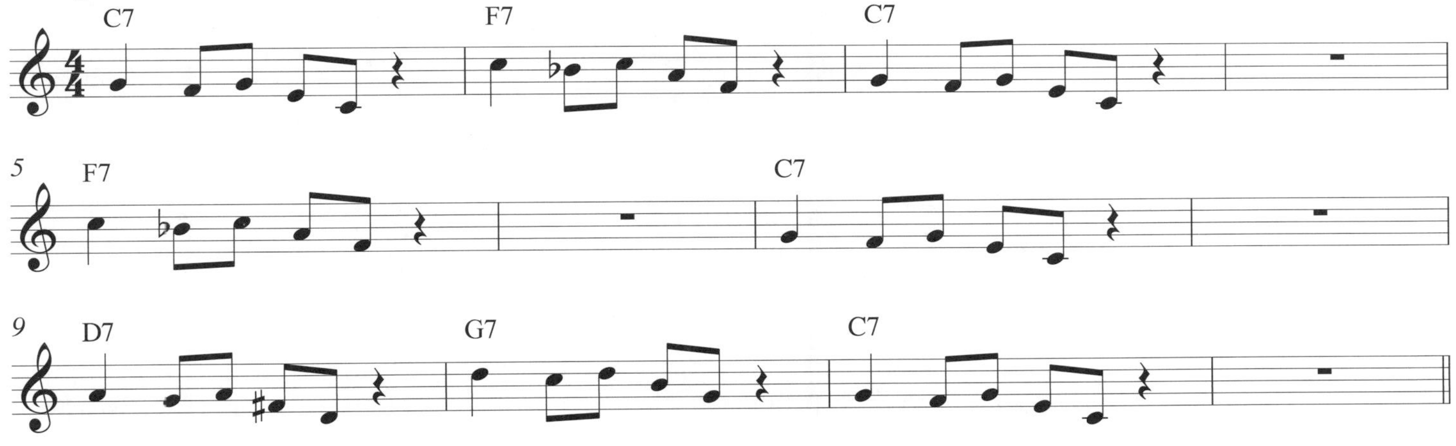

C7
F7
C7
5
F7
C7
9
D7
G7
C7

Example 2

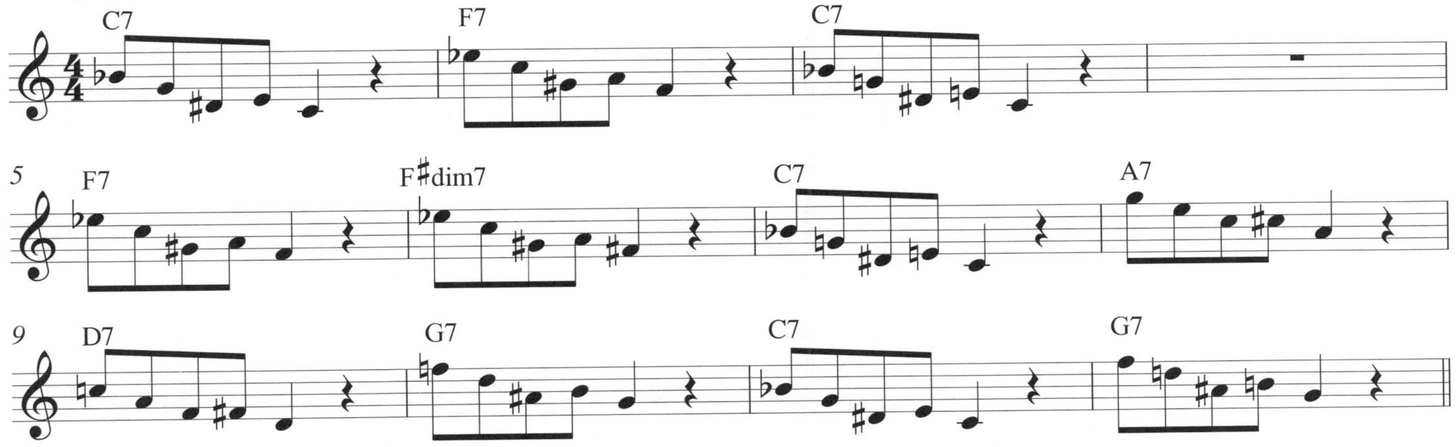

C7
F7
C7
5
F7
F♯dim7
C7
A7
9
D7
G7
C7
G7

Example 3

MAJOR/MINOR 3rd RIFFS

This section will focus on riffs that use an alternating major 3rd (M3) or minor 3rd (m3) of the key. To understand why, let's take a look at the voice leading.

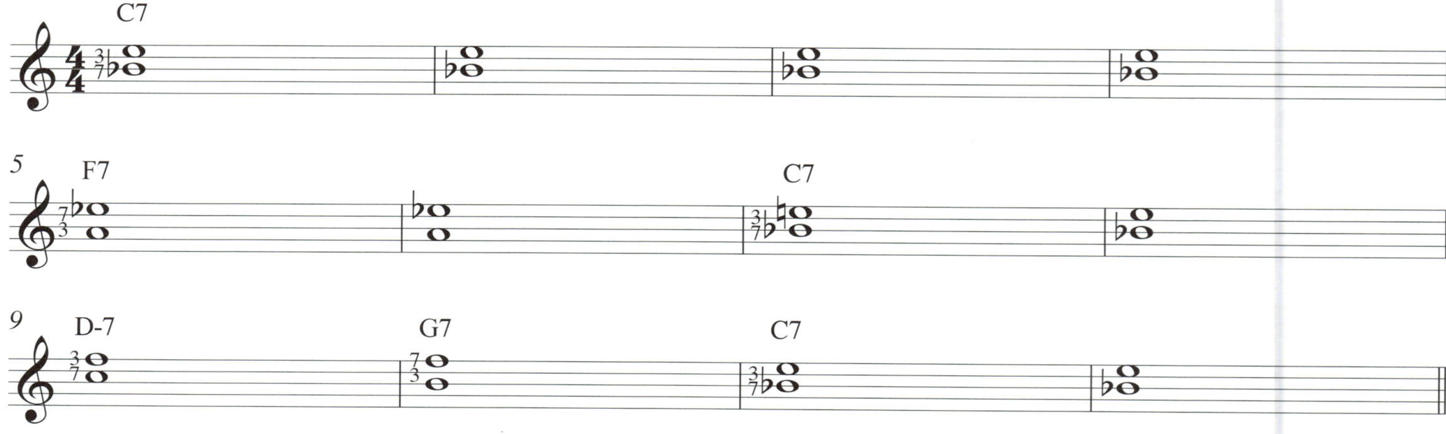

The example above shows the 3rds and 7ths in a 12-bar blues. Notice that bars 5-6 require the use of an E♭ because of the F7 chord. The two examples that follow offer several instances of melodies that use riffs with a major 3rd (M3). In each, the 3rd becomes minor in bars 5-6.

Example 1

RHYTHM CHANGES

Rhythms Changes is another important progression you should know. (We will study this in greater depth in Chapter 14.) It takes its name and chord progression from George Gershwin's song "I Got Rhythm." Many tunes are based on this progression, and there are many variations. We can approach the use of riffs over rhythm changes several different ways. The following is an example of typical 32-bar rhythm changes.

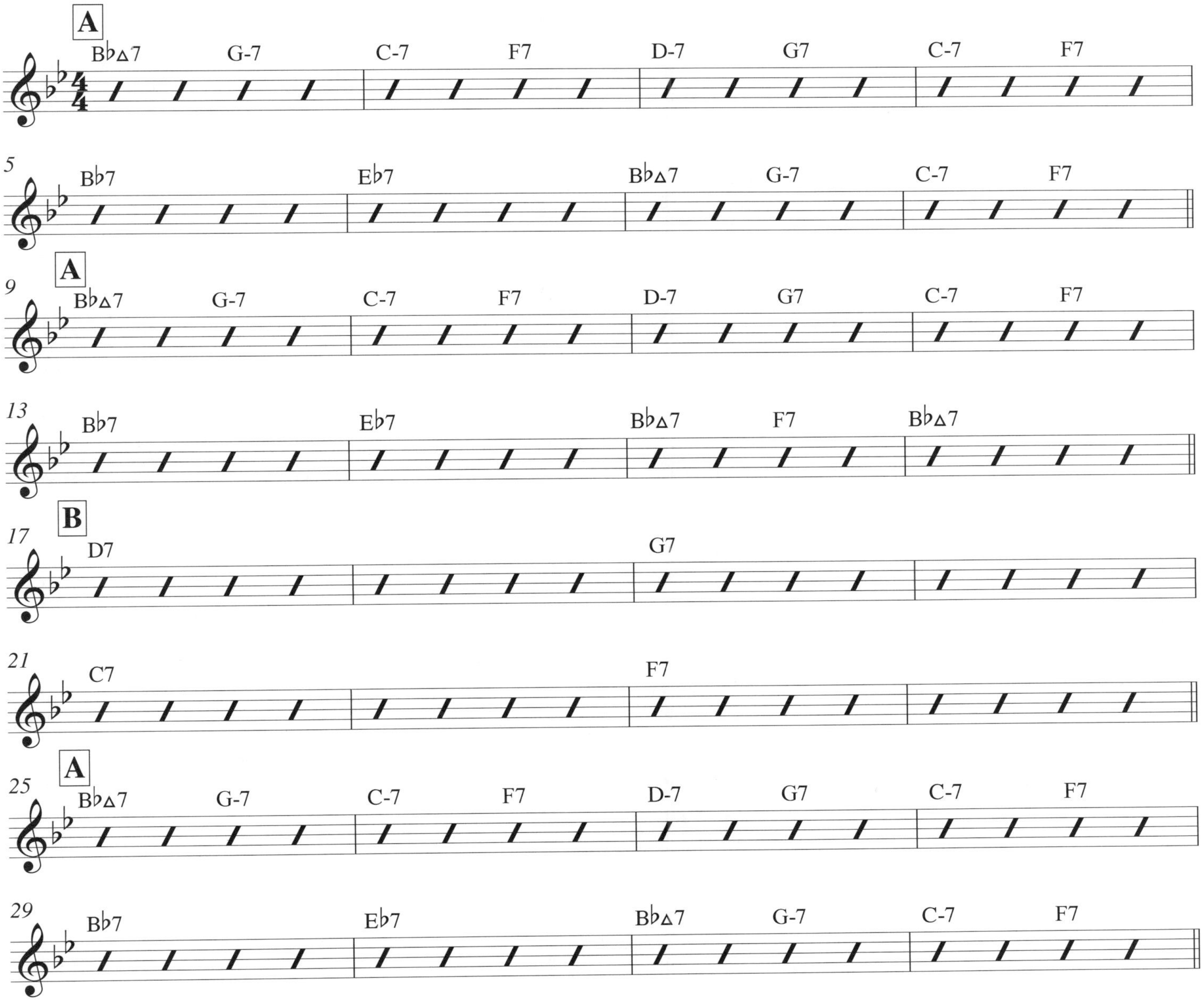

Section	Bar	Chords			
A	1	B♭Δ7 G-7	C-7 F7	D-7 G7	C-7 F7
	5	B♭7	E♭7	B♭Δ7 G-7	C-7 F7
A	9	B♭Δ7 G-7	C-7 F7	D-7 G7	C-7 F7
	13	B♭7	E♭7	B♭Δ7 F7	B♭Δ7
B	17	D7		G7	
	21	C7		F7	
A	25	B♭Δ7 G-7	C-7 F7	D-7 G7	C-7 F7
	29	B♭7	E♭7	B♭Δ7 G-7	C-7 F7

In the example that follows, concentration is placed on the I and IV chords within the A sections; the B section remains "as is."

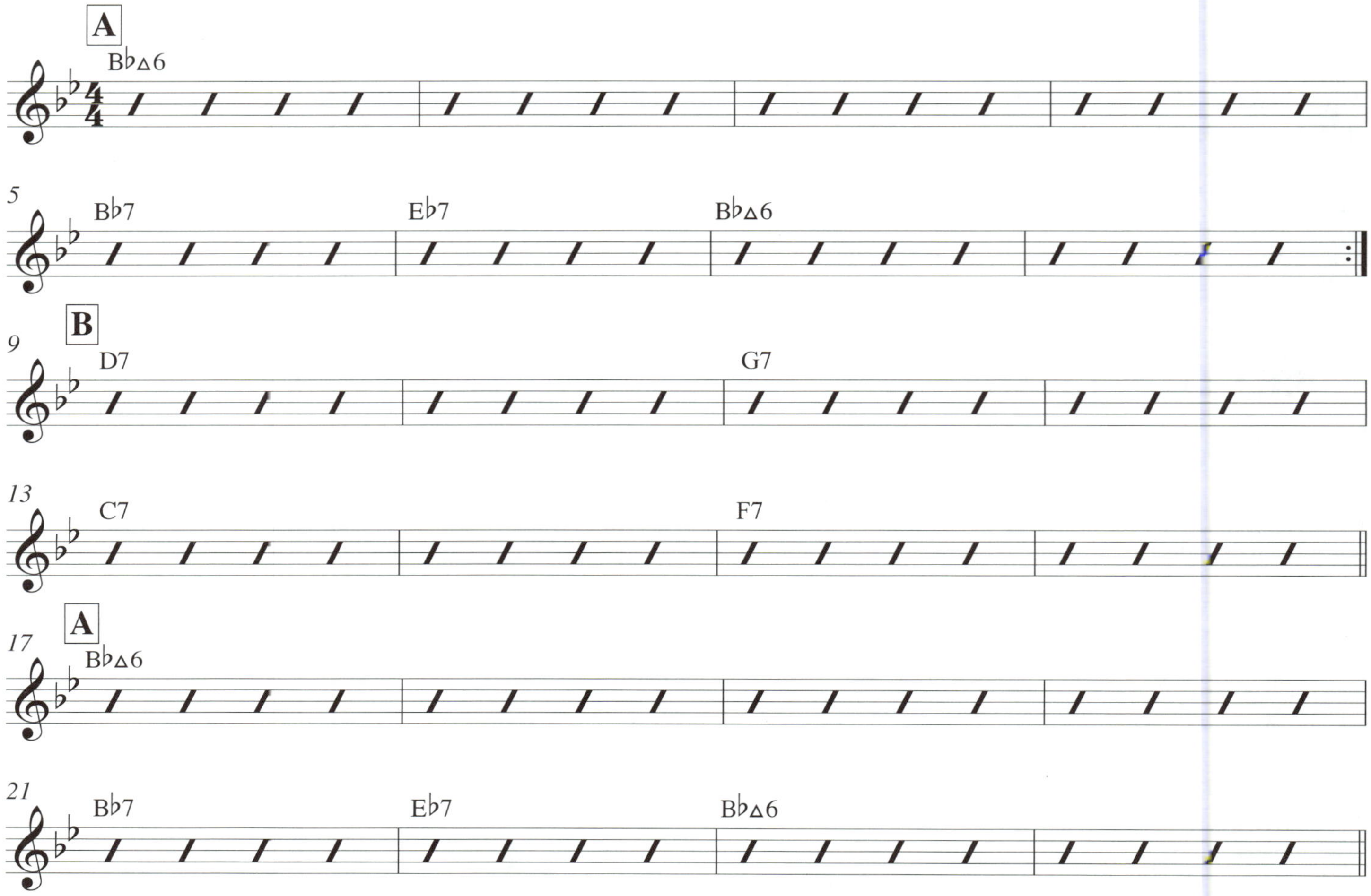

A

B♭△6

B♭7 E♭7 B♭△6

B

D7 G7

C7 F7

A

B♭△6

B♭7 E♭7 B♭△6

In the first four bars of the form, the chord B♭6 is used; in bar 5, a B♭7 chord. Technically, B♭7 serves as a V in the key of E♭ (the IV of the upcoming key). It is common for the I7 of any key to be used to transition to the IV of a key.

The following example uses the Kansas City Scale exclusively in the A sections, while chord riffs are used in the B section.

13
C7
F7
A
17
B♭△6
21
B♭7
E♭7
B♭△6

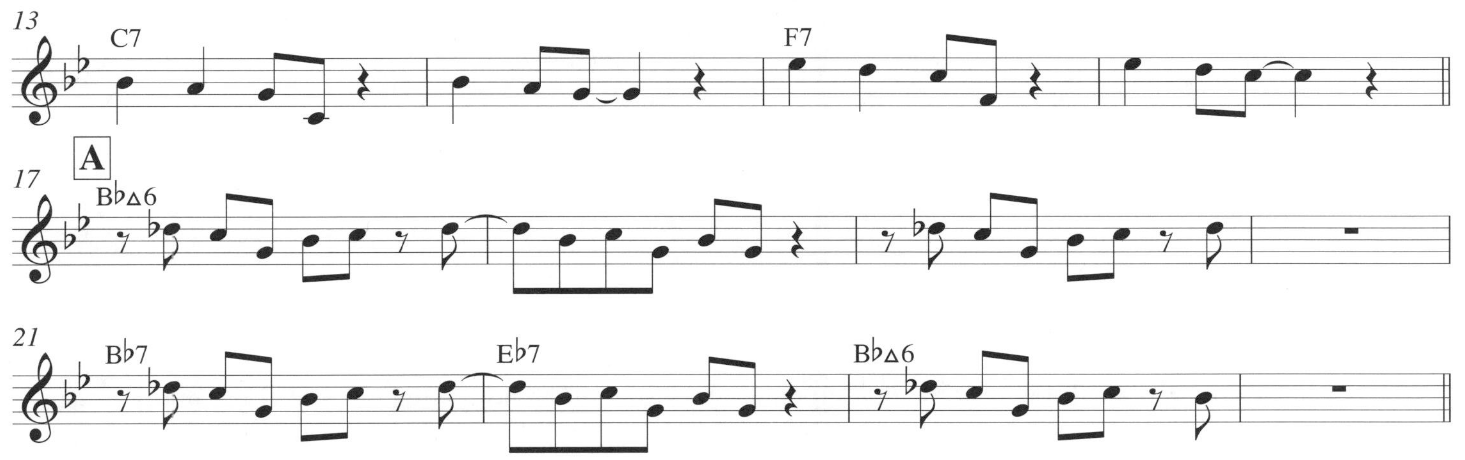

This example implements chord riffs that outline the sound of a customized Rhythm Changes form.

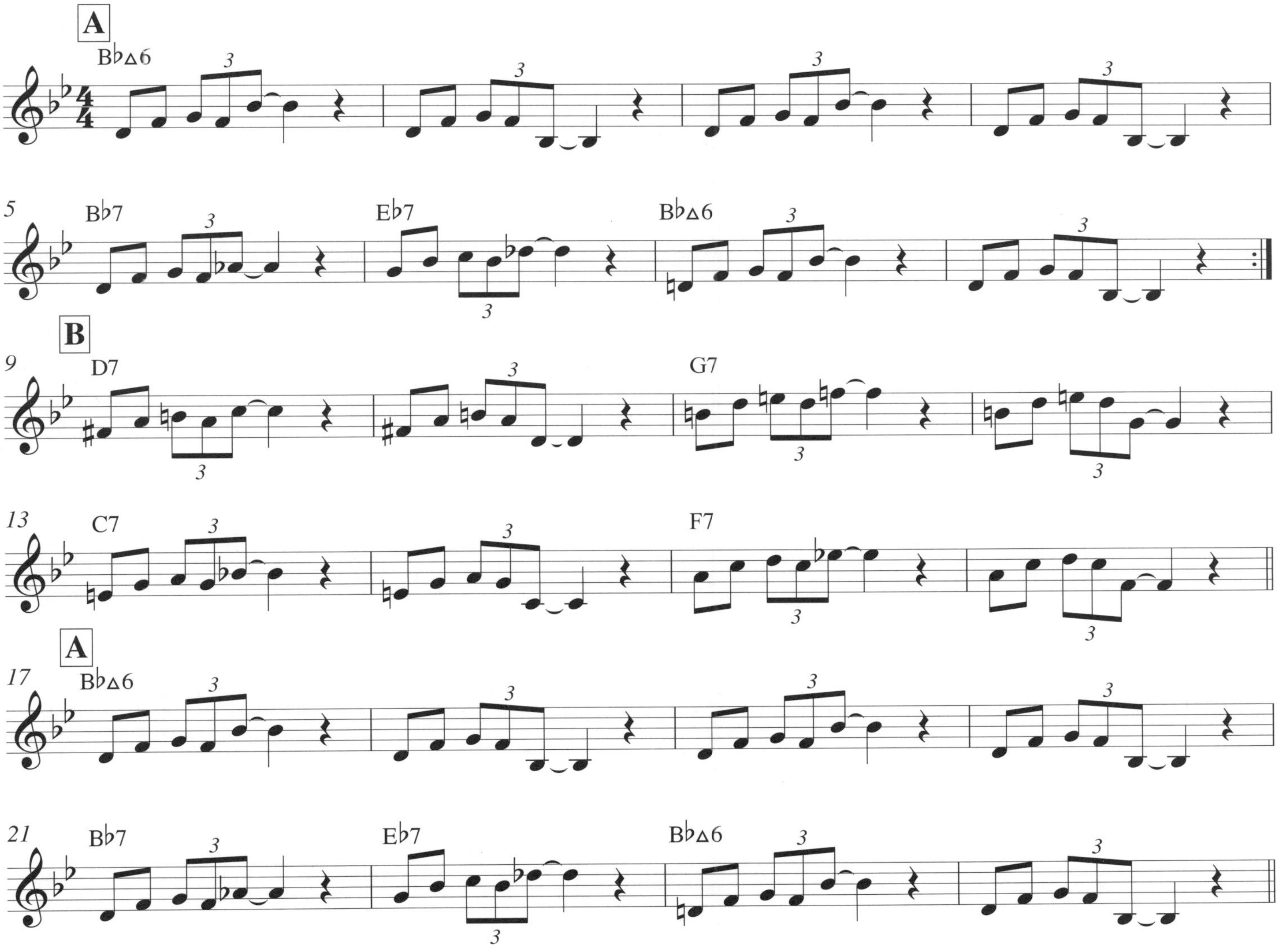
A
B♭△6
5
B♭7
E♭7
B♭△6
B
9
D7
G7
13
C7
F7
A
17
B♭△6
21
B♭7
E♭7
B♭△6

CHAPTER 3

BLUES SCALE & PENTATONIC SCALES

Concepts, Scales, and Modes

- 12-Bar Blues Revisited
- Blues Scale Revisited
- Pentatonic Scales
- Canvas Approach

In this chapter, we will identify the major pentatonic scale, the minor pentatonic scale, the blues scale, and the "blue note." Then we'll apply the scales over the 12-bar blues progression. Regular repetition of these exercises will increase your dexterity and augment your ability to hear and relate to the chords and scales. Developing aural correlations is as important as developing technical facility. Practice these scales in every key. Do not move on to other exercises until you have mastered each concept. You can do it!

ABOUT THE BLUES

The *blues* is both a musical form and a music genre. It was created at the end of the 19th century by African-Americans whose communities were located predominantly in the Deep South of the United States. It has origins including, but not limited to, spirituals, work songs, and field hollers. The blues has become synonymous with jazz, rhythm and blues, rock and roll, and other musical forms.

The blues (as a form) can be identified by its specific chord progression. The traditional 12-bar blues is perhaps the most common. It also is identified (both in genre and in form) through the use of *blue notes*, specific tones that for expressive purposes are altered, bent, or modified in relation to the notes found in the major scale.

12-Bar Blues Revisited

On page 15, we outlined the 12-bar blues in C major. In the key of B♭ major, the tonic chord is B♭, the subdominant chord is E♭, and the dominant chord is F. The example below shows a traditional 12-bar blues in B♭ major.

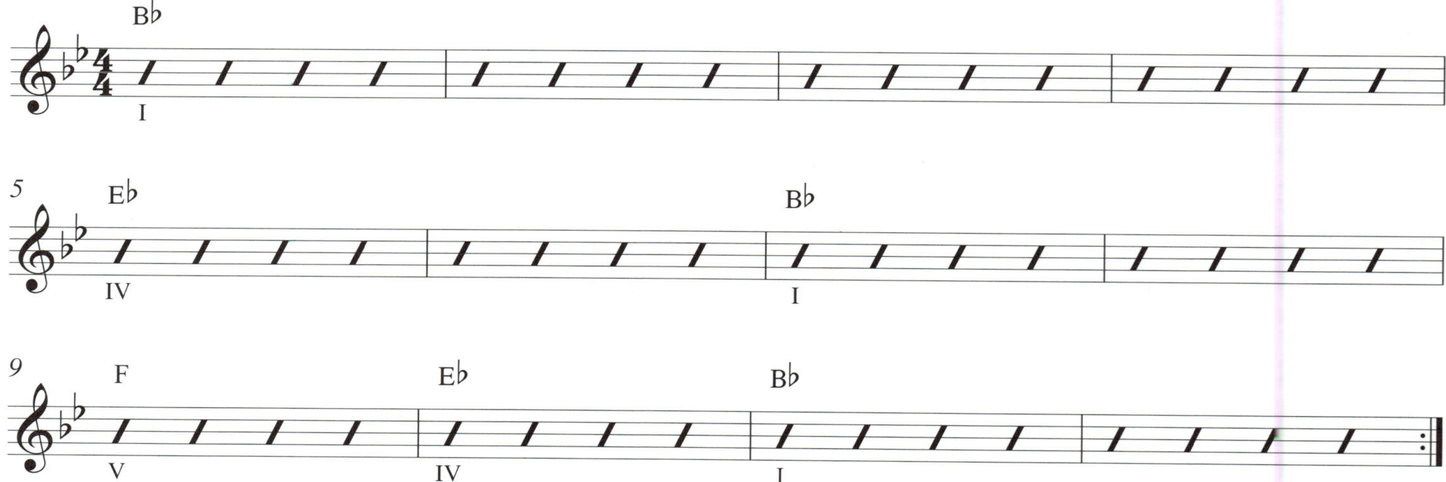

The 12-Bar Blues in Jazz Improvisation

In a jazz blues, chords progressions not only provide core functions (including subdominant, dominant, and tonic), but also furnish transitional material between sections. While a traditional blues is all in one key, a jazz blues has numerous key centers and navigates to and from different keys.

Each chord in a jazz blues is an "extended chord" – usually, a 7th chord at least (e.g., C7, F7, B♭7, etc.). This is part of the characteristic blues sound. Chords used in a 12-bar jazz blues can be observed in the following example, which includes Roman numeral analysis.

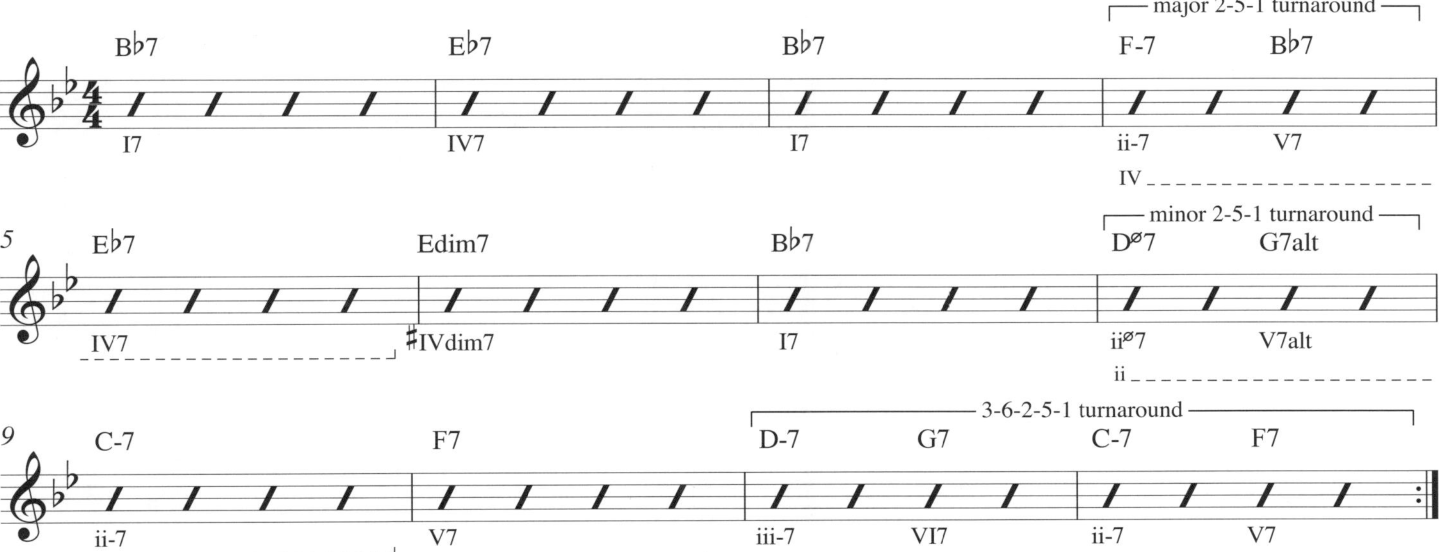

MAJOR PENTATONIC SCALE

On page 12, we referenced the major pentatonic scale in connection with the Kansas City Scale. The major pentatonic scale is one of the scales that can be used in the blues, a five-note scale created by using scale degrees 1, 2, 3, 5, and 6 of the major scale. In the key of B♭ major, for example, this scale consists of the notes B♭ (1)–C (2)–D (3)–F (5)–G (6).

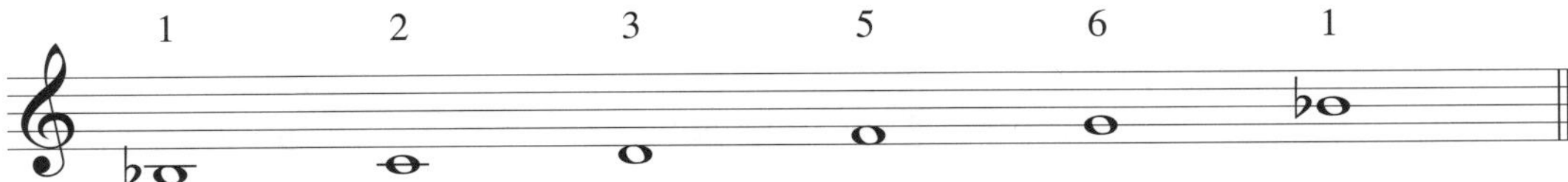

MINOR PENTATONIC SCALE

The minor pentatonic scale is another of the scales that can be used in the blues. This is a five-note scale created by using scale degrees 1, 3, 4, 5, and 7 of the natural minor scale. In the key of B♭ minor, for example, this scale consists of the notes B♭ (1)–D♭ (3)–E♭ (4)–F (5)–A♭ (7).

Recommendations

- Practice the minor pentatonic scale in every key, then play it around the Circle of 4ths (or 5ths).
- For fretted string players, the minor pentatonic scale should be practiced on one string, across the fingerboard in one position, and with a "shift."
- Keyboard players should learn the minor pentatonic scale, hands together, across two octaves.

THE BLUE NOTE

The blue note is used for expressivity within the blues. When compared to a major scale, the blue note can be found one half step higher than the fourth degree (♯11) or one half step lower than the fifth degree (♭5). In the key of C major, this note is F♯/G♭. In the key of F major, the blue note (B) can be found one half step above B♭ (the fourth scale degree) or one half step below C (the fifth scale degree). In B♭, the blue note is F♭ (♭5) or E♮ (♯11), as shown below.

THE BLUES SCALE REVISITED

In Chapter 2 (page 13), we learned about the blues scale in the key of C. Let's expand on that a bit. Remember this formula: the blue note + minor pentatonic scale = the blues scale. In the key of B♭, shown above, the blues scale is spelled B♭ (1)–D♭ (♭3)–E♭ (4)–F♭/E (blue note)–F (5)–A♭ (♭7).

The addition of the blue note also gives the blues scale its character (or "blue tonality"), a sound common to other genres influenced by the blues. It provides chromaticism (stepwise movement between notes in half steps) and changes the relationship between the fourth and fifth scale degrees by placing the blue note in between the third and fourth note of the minor pentatonic scale.

Recommendations

- Learn the blues scale in every key, then play it around the Circle of 4ths (or 5ths).
- For fretted string players, the blues scale should be learned on one string, across the fingerboard in one position, and with a "shift."
- Keyboard players should learn the blues scale, hands together, across two octaves.

PLAYING THE BLUES: CANVAS APPROACH

The canvas approach to improvisation allows you to focus on a singular idea, pattern, scale, mode, or rhythm and apply it in a larger context. This limitation can be implemented in a number of ways – for a section of a piece, or even for an entire song. An example of a canvas approach is using the blues scale as a basis for improvisation, because all the notes work within the B♭ blues tonality. The blues scale can be played over the entire blues form. Here, we use the blues scale shown above.

PLAYING THE BLUES: CANVAS APPROACH USING MINOR PENTATONIC SCALES

The minor pentatonic scale (the fifth mode of the major pentatonic scale) provides the opportunity for improvisers to play in an intervallic, pattern-oriented manner. Just as the blues scale can be played over the entire blues form, so can the minor pentatonic scale. Here, we use the one shown on page 23.

CHAPTER SUPPLEMENT

Eight Ways to Play a Pattern

To expand your melodic and harmonic vocabulary, apply a set of notes in as many ways as possible. You can facilitate this process through the use of patterns – musical phrases constructed in two- to six-note motifs that encapsulate a single musical idea. Patterns can be used for beginning and ending phrases, to extend harmonic/melodic ideas, to ascend and/or descend chords, to navigate phrases, and so on. Most patterns are based on scales. Each time you learn a pattern, you'll have an opportunity to utilize it in various guises. Here are eight different ways to play a single pattern. Notated examples are shown on page 27.

- **ascending:** rising motif
- **retrograde:** motif played with notes descending/backward
- **inverted ascending:** descending motif played ascending
- **inverted retrograde:** ascending motif played descending/backward
- **alternating ascending:** ascending motif followed by a descending motif (ascending version)
- **alternating retrograde:** descending motif followed by ascending motif (descending version)
- **inverted alternating ascending:** inverted motif followed by inverted retrograde motif (ascending version)
- **inverted alternating retrograde:** inverted motif followed by inverted retrograde motif (descending version)

In this text, you'll have the opportunity to practice patterns attached to the history and tradition of jazz performance, and to use these patterns to create your own ideas.

Helpful Tips

1. Learn each pattern all eight ways.
2. Learn each pattern in all 12 keys.
3. Practice each pattern in different ways; e.g., displace it by an eighth note, change the rhythm, change the accents.
4. Practice each pattern over the full range of the instrument.

Ascending
etc.
Retrograde
etc.
Inverted Ascending
etc.
Inverted Retrograde
etc.
Alternating Ascending
etc.
Alternating Retrograde
etc.
Inverted Alternating Ascending
etc.
Inverted Alternating Retrograde
etc.

CHAPTER 4

WORKING WITH MODES

Concepts, Scales, and Modes

- Modes (new)
- Canvas Approach (review)
- 12-Bar Blues (review)
- Blues Scale (review)
- Minor Pentatonic Scale (review)

In this chapter, we will identify the modes derived from the major scale and then apply those modes in the 12-bar blues progression. You will play exercises that will develop your ability to associate each mode with a chord type. Regular repetition of these exercises will increase your dexterity and augment your ability to hear and relate to the chord progression.

Playing the blues – or any sort of tune, really – is not just about executing the right notes or patterns, but also about making musical sense of what is heard around you. Developing aural correlations with the sonority of blues chords and the sounds of modes is as important as developing technical facility. Delve into the exercises and master all the concepts. You can do it!

ABOUT THE MODES

Each mode is created by starting on a different note of the major scale. Each of these modes can then be applied to corresponding chord types.

There are seven modes that can be derived from a major scale. They are:

- Ionian maj7
- Dorian m7
- Phrygian m7♭13(♭9)
- Lydian maj7♯11
- Mixolydian m7
- Aeolian m7♭13
- Locrian m7♭13(♭9, ♭5)

For example, C major yields seven different modes.

- C Ionian Cmaj7
- D Dorian Dm7
- E Phrygian Em7♭13(♭9)
- F Lydian Fmaj7♯11
- G Mixolydian G7
- A Aeolian Am7♭13
- B Locrian Bm7♭13(♭9, ♭5)

This method can be applied to every major scale. Twelve major scales multiplied by seven modes yields 84 scales. (12 x 7 = 84)

Recommendations

- Learn the modes in every key, then play each around the Circle of 4ths (or 5ths).
- Play all the modes starting on the same note; e.g., C Ionian, C Dorian, C Phrygian, etc. (See page 33.)
- For fretted string players, each scale should be learned on one string, across the fingerboard in one position, and with a "shift."
- Keyboard players should learn each mode, hands together, across two octaves.
- Percussionists should follow keyboard standards, using mallet instruments, or learn on keyboard).
- Focus on the unique sound of each mode.

The following chart shows the seven modes derived from the C major scale.

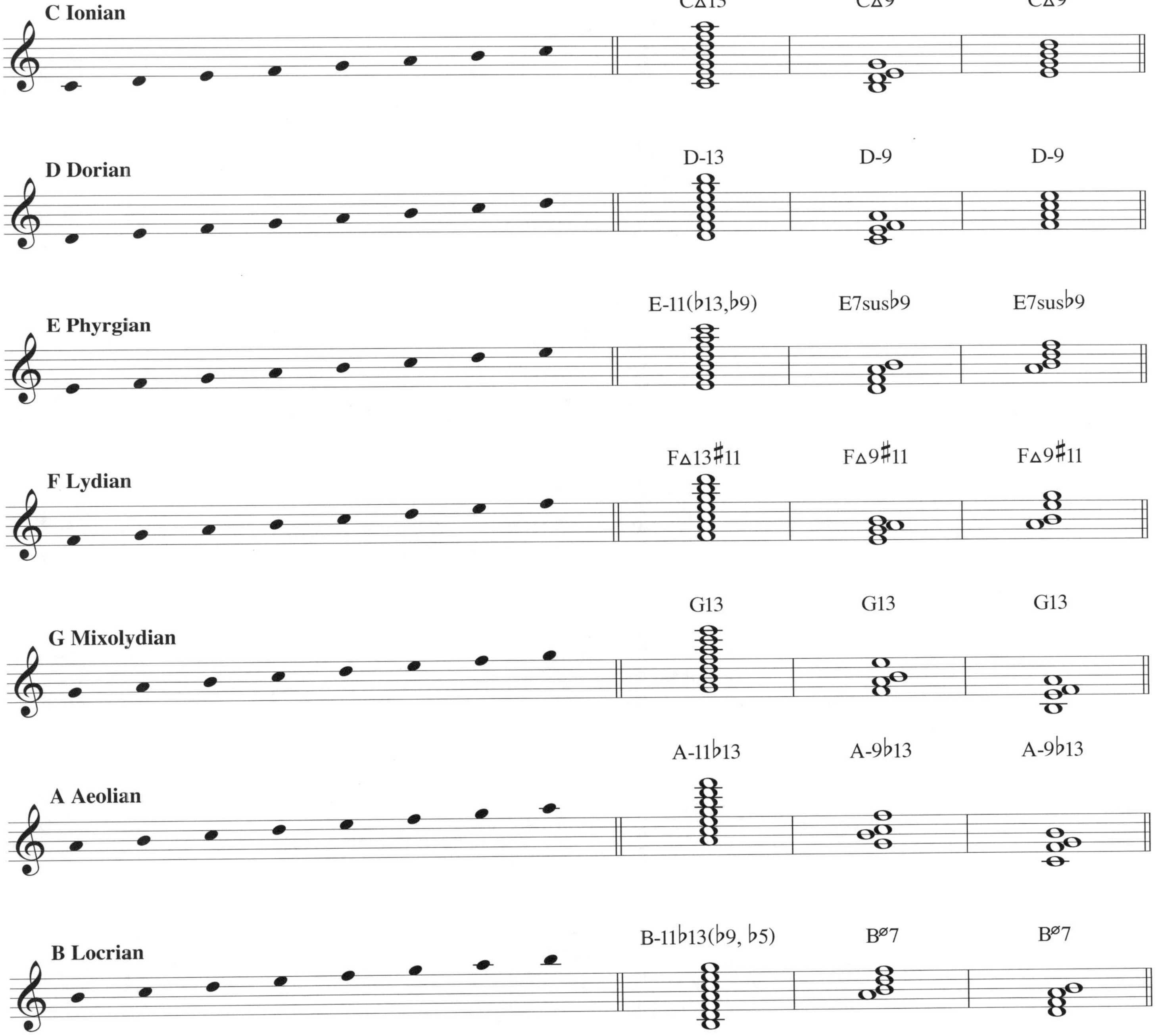

MODES APPLIED TO THE BLUES PROGRESSION

Applying modes within the blues can provide you with a solid base from which to create a plethora of melodies, shapes, and patterns while maintaining consonance with each chord. This is a core principle of chord-scale theory, a practice in which each chord has a corresponding scale or mode. (See Chapter 1, page 5.)

In the following example, we apply a mode to each measure of the blues progression. The notes are diatonic to each chord-scale relationship.

- **measure 1:** B♭7 = B♭ Mixolydian
- **measure 2:** E♭7 = E♭ Mixolydian
- **measure 3:** B♭7 = B♭ Mixolydian
- **measure 4:** Fm7, B♭7 = F Dorian , B♭ Mixolydian
- **measure 5:** E♭7 = E♭ Mixolydian
- **measure 6:** Edim7 = E diminished (not a major mode)
- **measure 7:** B♭7 = B♭ Mixolydian
- **measure 8:** Dø7 (half-diminished), G13♯11(♯9, ♭9) = D Locrian, G Phrygian
- **measure 9:** Cm7 = C Dorian
- **measure 10:** F7 = F Mixolydian
- **measure 11:** Dm7, G7 = D Dorian, G Mixolydian
- **measure 12:** Cm7, F7 = C Dorian, F Mixolydian

MODES FOR THE BLUES (FULL OCTAVE SCALES)

* For this measure, Dorian and Mixolydian share the same notes.
** For this measure, Locrian and Phrygian share the same notes.

In the four exercises that follow, practice slowly at first, using a metronome. Over time, work toward ♩ = 120.

Modes for the Blues – Ascending

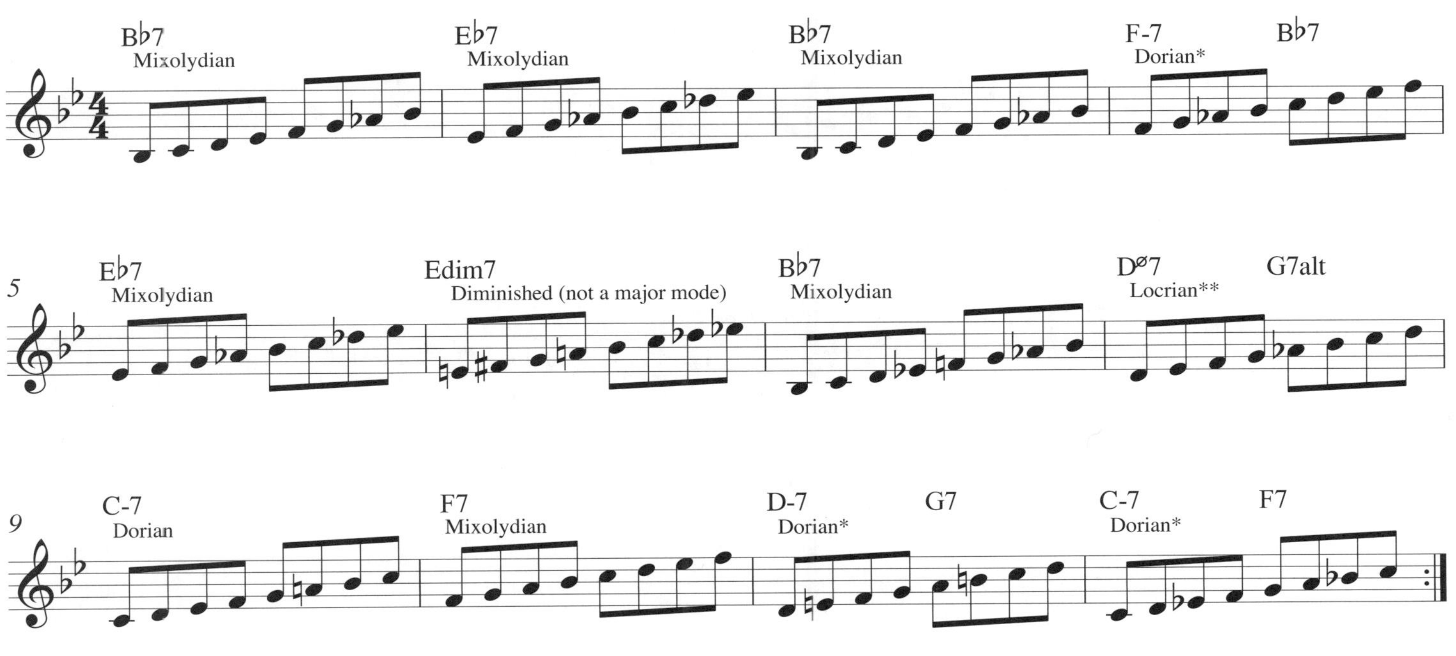

Modes for the Blues – Descending

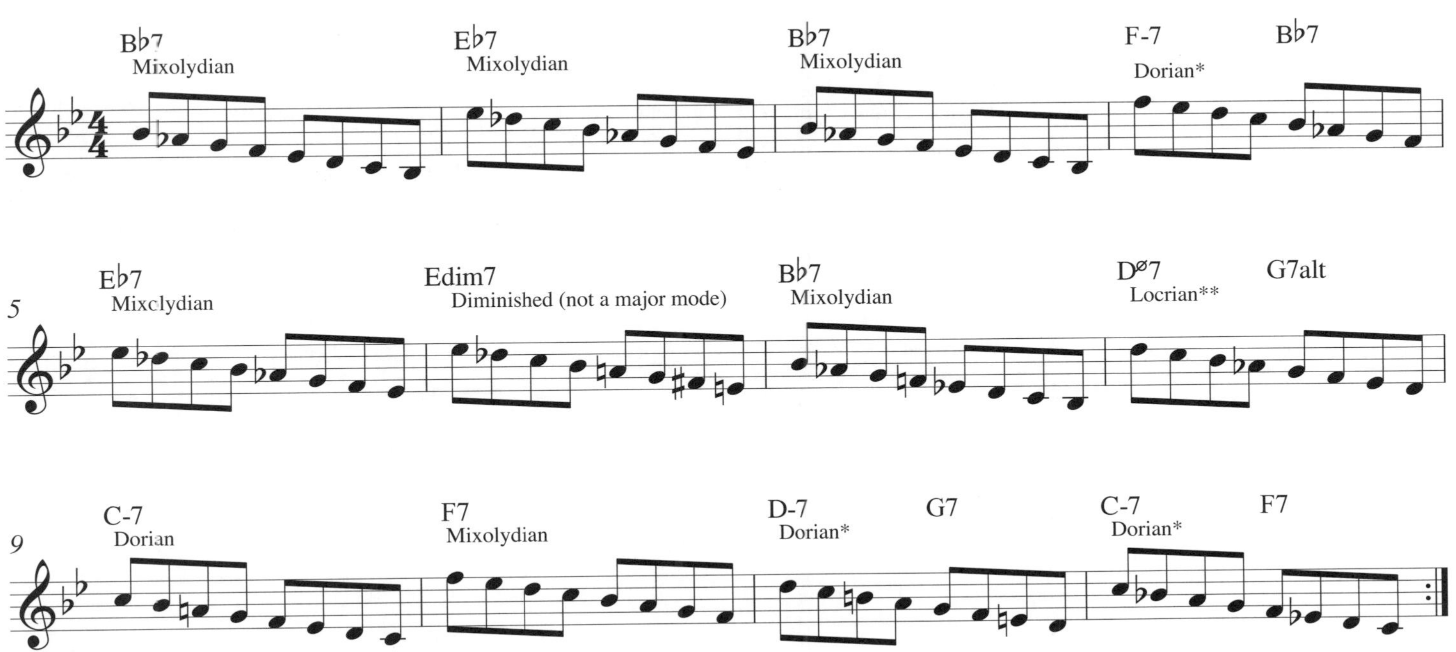

* For this measure, Dorian and Mixolydian share the same notes.
** For this measure, Locrian and Phrygian share the same notes.

Modes for the Blues – Alternating (A)

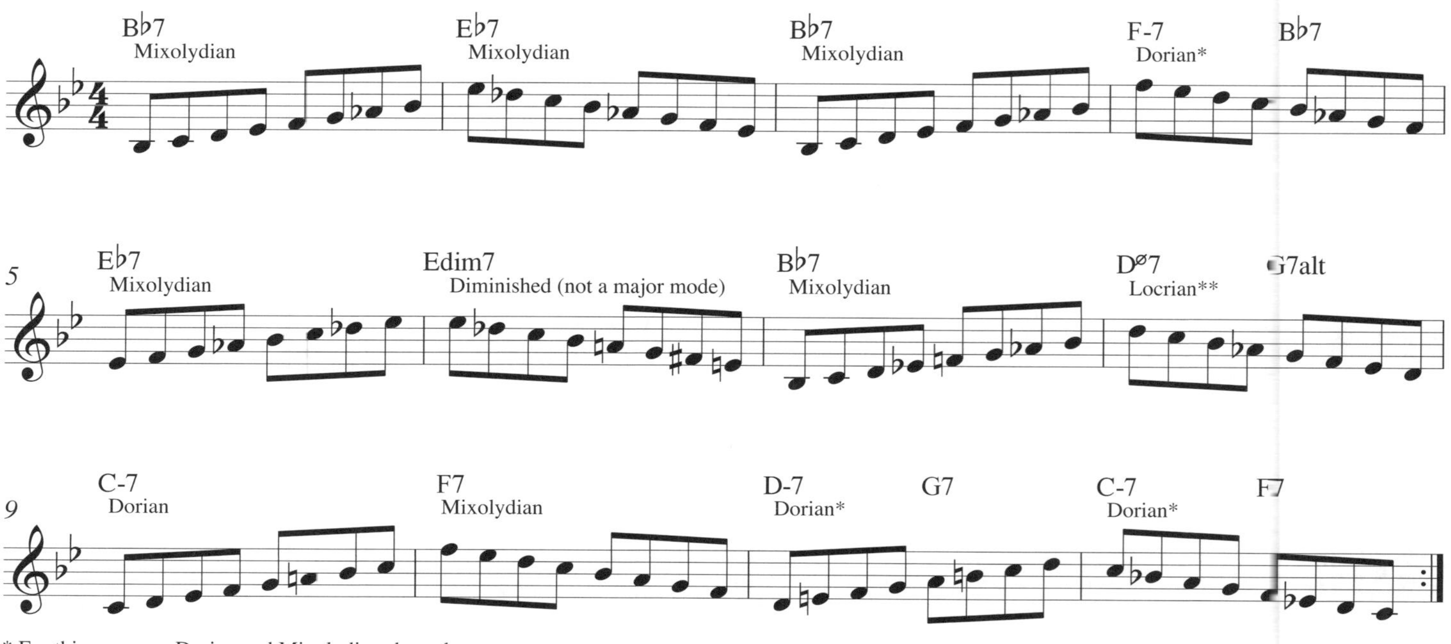

* For this measure, Dorian and Mixolydian share the same notes.
** For this measure, Locrian and Phrygian share the same notes.

Modes for the Blues – Alternating (B)

* For this measure, Dorian and Mixolydian share the same notes.
** For this measure, Locrian and Phrygian share the same notes.

CHAPTER SUPPLEMENT

Unison and Diatonic Relationships

The study of chords and scales is the foundation of jazz harmony. These relationships can be handled two different ways: unison and diatonic.

Unison Relationships: Chords and scales are compared to each other from the root, usually starting with the major key. For example, C major:

Major	C	D	E	F	G	A	B
	1	2	3	4	5	6	7
Dorian	C	D	E♭	F	G	A	B♭
	1	2	♭3	4	5	♭6 (♭13)	7
Phrygian	C	D♭	E♭	F	G	A♭	B♭
	1	♭2	♭3	4	5	♭6	♭7
Lydian	C	D	E	F♯	G	A	B
	1	2	3	♯4 (♯11)	5	6	7
Mixolydian	C	D	E	F	G	A	B♭
	1	2	3	4	5	6	♭7
Aeolian	C	D	E♭	F	G	A♭	B♭
	1	2	♭3	4	5	♭6 (♭13)	♭7
Locrian	C	D♭	E♭	F	G♭	A♭	B♭
	1	♭2	♭3	4	♭5	♭6 (♭13)	♭7

Diatonic Relationships: Chords and scales are derived from the notes diatonic to that chord's root or scale's root. For example, C major:

Major	C	D	E	F	G	A	B
	1	2	3	4	5	6	7
Dorian	D	E	F	G	A	B	C
	2	3	4	5	6	7	1
Phrygian	E	F	G	A	B	C	D
	3	4	5	6	7	1	2
Lydian	F	G	A	B	C	D	E
	4	5	6	7	1	2	3
Mixolydian	G	A	B	C	D	E	F
	5	6	7	1	2	3	4
Aeolian	A	B	C	D	E	F	G
	6	7	1	2	3	4	5
Locrian	B	C	D	E	F	G	A
	7	1	2	3	4	5	6

In this text, both approaches – creating chords and scales from unison and diatonic relationships – are implemented. Both methods are important for development, in order to recognize scales and modes aurally, to relate modes with key centers, and to train the brain to make both the aural and theoretical connections to the tonality.

The diatonic approach to modes, with C major as the reference scale, is notated on page 29. The unison approach, with the pitch C as the starting note for the seven modes, is notated below.

Modes – Unison

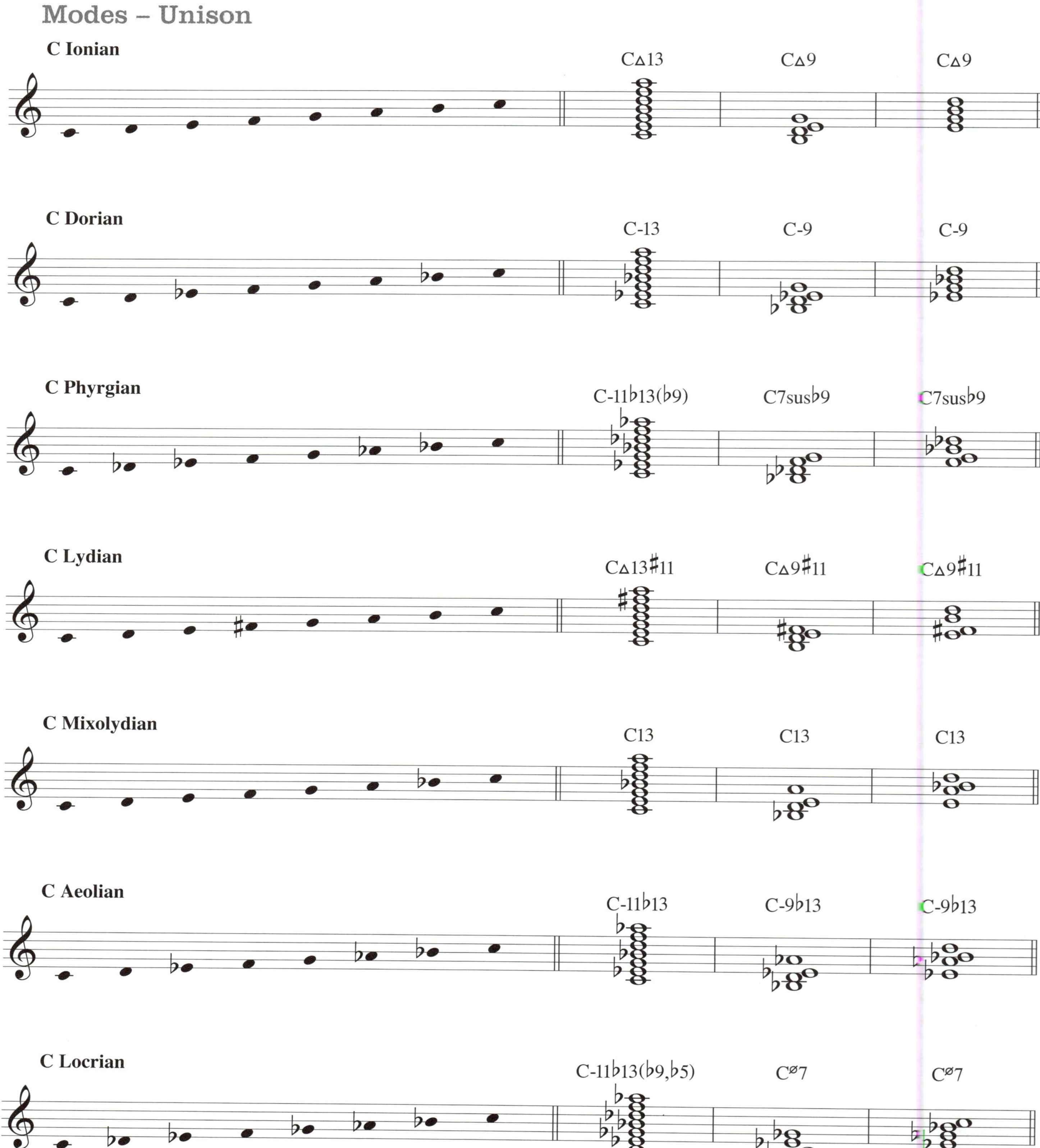

CHAPTER 5

CONTINUOUS SCALES & DIATONIC TRANSPOSITION

Concepts, Scales, and Modes

- Continuous Scales
- Diatonic Transposition

In this chapter, you will refine your ability to play the blues through the use of two concepts: 1) continuous scales; 2) diatonic transposition. Using continuous scales, you'll concentrate on linear playing by limiting yourself to stepwise motion. Diatonic transposition will expand your vocabulary by taking a single phrase (or motif), then altering it to fit the new key. The concepts here will help you develop aural correlations with the sound of scales and patterns as well as develop your technical facility. **Remember:** Do not move on to other exercises until you have mastered each concept. You can do it!

ABOUT CONTINUOUS SCALES

The term *continuous scale* refers to the practice of applying stepwise motion across an entire chord progression. This practice removes wider intervals from the improvisation and forces the player to develop linear ideas. Practice the example below, a 12-bar blues in B♭ major.

Rhythmically, a continuous scale can be created using half notes, quarter notes, eighth notes, 16th notes, and – if you want an even greater challenge – 32nd notes. In this text, continuous scales are constructed using eighth notes. Harmonically, all other notes used in continuous scales in this text will function with the harmonic structure and the chords of a 12-bar blues.

If using church modes, only whole steps and half steps can be used and notes may not be repeated. If using minor pentatonic, harmonic minor, or augmented scales, larger intervals can be used, but only where the intervals already exist in each scale.

Continuous scales take you beyond simply knowing the scales that fit on each chord. Instead, you must apply scales in a manner that allows you to continue from notes played in the previous measure without jumping back to the root of the chord, unless the root is a whole step or half step away from the previous note. Continuous scales will help you improve linear playing, and also will encourage you to eliminate root bias. Instead of jumping from root to root, you can establish strong stepwise connections between chords.

After playing the exercises, try to write – and then improvise – your own continuous scales. Here are some guidelines:

- Each note may be only one half step or one whole step away from the previous note.
- Notes may not be repeated (i.e., playing a C immediately after playing a C).
- Do not return to the root of the chord unless the root is a half step or a whole step away from the previous note.
- Each note played must be within scales diatonic to each chord.

DIATONIC TRANSPOSITION

Diatonic transposition pertains to a series of notes (in a motif) altered by a new key signature. The shape and rhythm of the motif are maintained, but accidentals alter the notes. Practice each etude with a metronome, gradually increasing the tempo over a period of days and weeks. Work toward ♩ = 120.

BLUES MAJOR MODE DIATONIC TRANSPOSITION STUDIES

Transposition Study #1

Transposition Study #2A – Forward

Transposition Study #2B – Backward

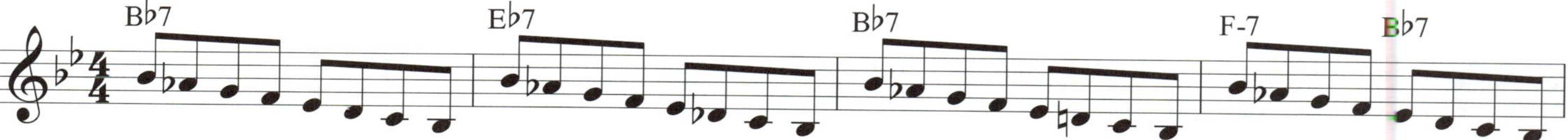

5
Eb7 Edim7 Bb7 Dø7 G7sus(b9)
9
C-7 F D-7 G7 C-7 F7
Transposition Study #2C – Alternating A
Bb7 Eb7 Bb7 F-7 Bb7
5
Eb7 Edim7 Bb7 Dø7 G7sus(b9)
9
C-7 F D-7 G7 C-7 F7
Transposition Study #2D – Alternating B
Bb7 Eb7 Bb7 F-7 Bb7
5
Eb7 Edim7 Bb7 Dø7 G7sus(b9)
9
C-7 F D-7 G7 C-7 F7
Transposition Study #3A – Ascending
Bb7 Eb7 Bb7 F-7 Bb7
5
Eb7 Edim7 Bb7 Dø7 G7sus(b9)
9
C-7 F D-7 G7 C-7 F7

Transposition Study #3B – Descending

Transposition Study #4A – Ascending

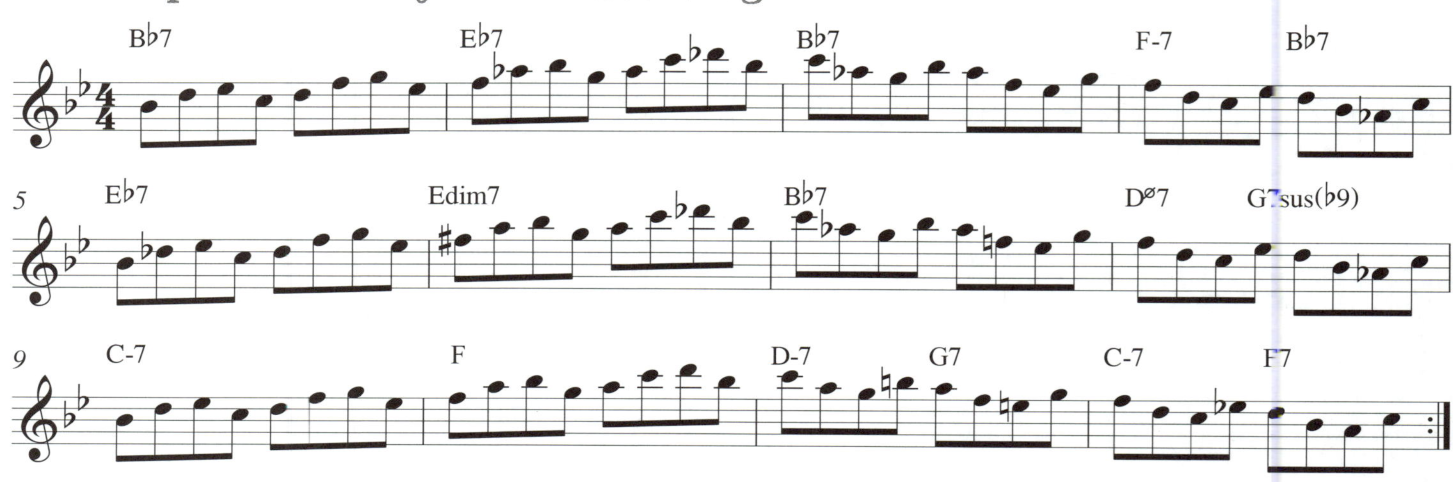

Transposition Study #4B – Descending

CHAPTER SUPPLEMENT

Concept Review

This etude brings together the concepts we've worked on previously. Using your trusty metronome, start slowly, increasing the tempo over time. If you make mistakes, opt for an even slower speed.

CHAPTER 6

3rds & 7ths | ARPEGGIOS

Concepts, Scales, and Modes

- 3rds and 7ths within chords
- Arpeggios

In this chapter, you will expand your understanding of the blues by focusing on chord structure. The ability to hear the 3rd and 7th within a chord structure will help you identify the chord's quality. Arpeggios will aid in recognizing the four most important notes of each chord. The concepts presented here will serve to develop aural correlations with these chord qualities and increase your technical facility. **Remember:** Do not move on to other exercises until you have mastered each concept. You can do it!

CHORD TONES: THE 3rd AND THE 7th

Within a 7th chord, the 3rd and the 7th are essential in defining its quality; they serve as anchor points that improvisers use to shape melodic and/or rhythmic structures. The etude below shows the 3rds and 7ths of several chords used melodically. In bar 1, for example, D is the 3rd in a B♭7 chord; A♭ is the 7th. Play these four measures on your instrument.

The 3rd and the 7th are key components and serve as "target notes." You need to be familiar with the common 7th chord qualities.

Let's review some of the material covered in Chapter 1, but with a slightly different approach.

Major 7th Chords (maj7)

A major 7th chord has a root, major 3rd, perfect 5th, and major 7th – in other words, it is a major triad with a major 3rd added on top. It is the chord ordinarily used for tonic functions.

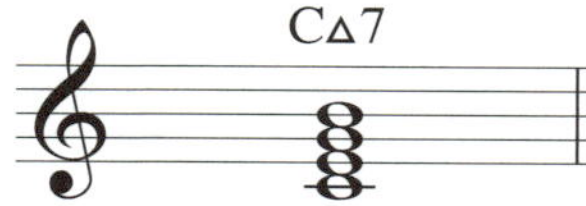

Dominant 7th Chords (V7)

A dominant 7th chord has a root, major 3rd, perfect 5th, and minor 7th – in other words, it is a major triad with a minor 7th. It is the chord most often met with in the blues, used for tonic, subdominant, and dominant functions.

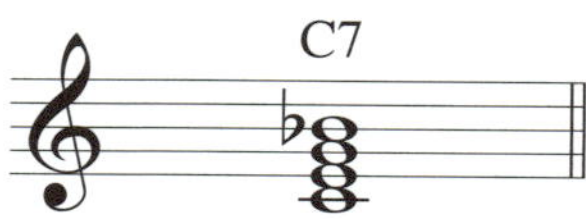

Minor 7th Chords (m7)

A minor 7th chord has a root, minor 3rd, perfect 5th, and minor 7th – in other words, it is a minor triad with a minor 7th. It is regularly found in the blues, in ii–V chord progressions, and serves a subdominant function.

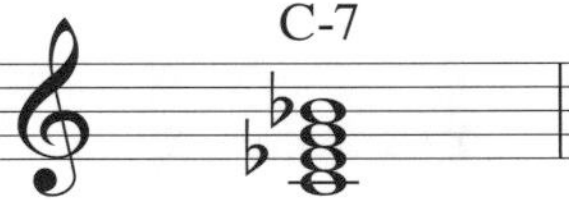

Half-Diminished 7th Chords (ø7)

A half-diminished 7th chord has a root, minor 3rd, ♭5th, and minor 7th – in other words, it is a diminished triad with a minor 7th. It is most commonly found in the blues as a transitional chord, and serves a subdominant function.

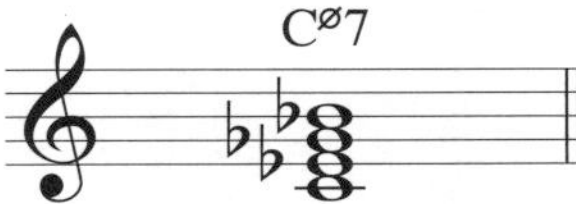

Fully-Diminished 7th Chords (dim7)

Fully-diminished 7th chords are constructed of superimposed minor 3rds. In the blues, a diminished 7th chord is used as a transitional chord. The spelling is root, minor 3rd, ♭5th, and diminished 7th.

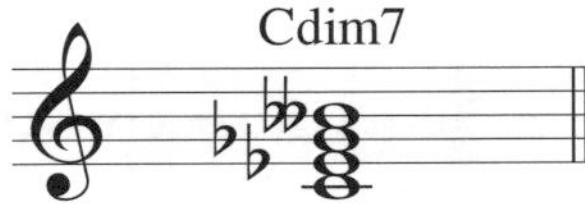

Working with 3rds and 7ths

When studying chord progressions, it's essential to know the 3rds and 7ths of each chord. Quick identification can help you make better note choices. There are several possible note choices, depending on the stated tonality; however, if you play the wrong 3rd or 7th – for example, minor 3rd instead of the major 3rd or ♭7th instead of the ♮7th – it will be obvious even to the untrained ear. The example below expands on the four-bar etude on page 40, showing the melodic use of the 3rds and 7ths of chords in a 12-bar blues.

ARPEGGIOS

An arpeggio is a group of notes belonging to one chord, played in sequence, either ascending or descending. In this method, arpeggios are built using the four most important notes of the chord – root, 3rd, 5th, and 7th. The following etude, in B♭ major, is a 12-bar blues consisting entirely of arpeggiated chords.

PLAYING EXERCISES

Practice each etude with a metronome, gradually increasing the tempo over a period of days and weeks. Work toward ♩ = 120.

Blues 3rds and 7ths – Backward

Blues 3rds and 7ths – Alternating (A)

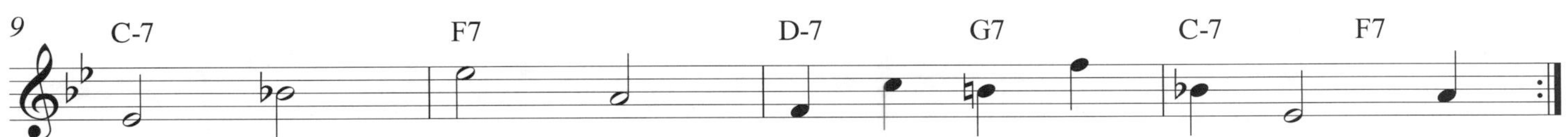

Blues 3rds and 7ths – Alternating (B)

B♭ Blues Arpeggio Study

B♭ Blues Arpeggio Study – Backward

B♭ Blues Arpeggio Study – Alternating (A)

B♭ Blues Arpeggio Study – Alternating (B)

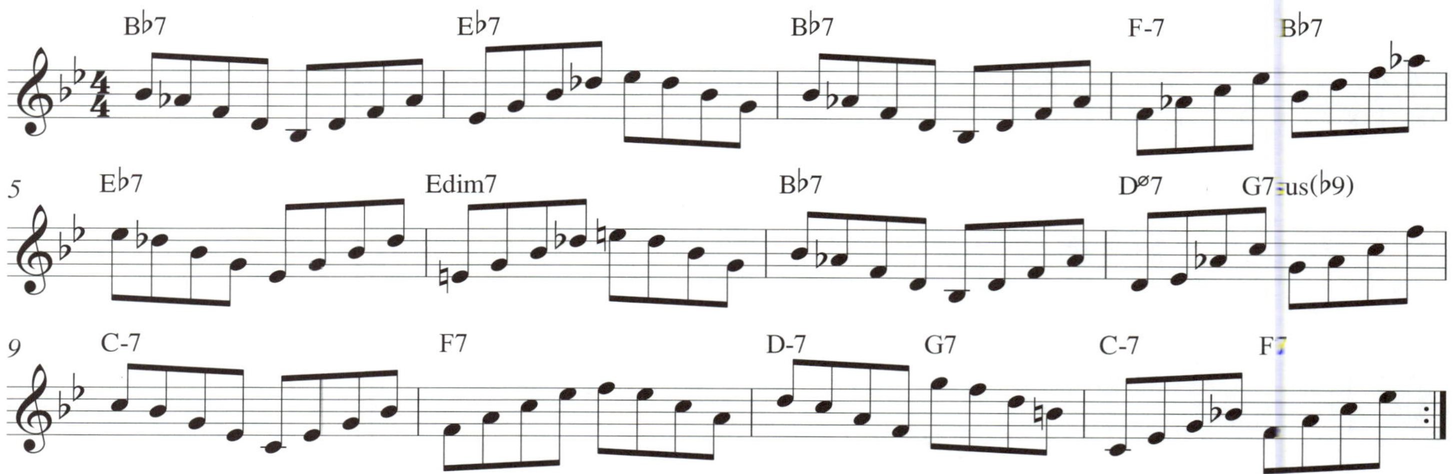

CHAPTER 7
CHROMATICISM

Concepts, Scales, and Modes

- Bebop Scales
- Leading Tones
- Enclosure

In this chapter, you will concentrate on chromaticism, including tension and half-step resolutions from non-chord tones to chord tones. The exercises here will teach you to make note choices that lead chromatically to the next chord in the sequence, and will help you develop aural skills and technical facility with enclosure and leading tones. **Remember:** Do not move on to other exercises until you have mastered each concept. You can do it!

CHROMATICISM

Chromaticism is a technique whereby the primary diatonic pitches and chords of a given key are interspersed with other pitches of the chromatic scale. These pitches, which are outside the stated tonality, are resolved via half step to notes within the diatonic scale. We can use the term "stated tonality" to refer to the key or mode diatonic to a chord or scale.

If the chord is Dm7, for example, you may choose to play notes from D Dorian Mode. The "stated tonality" is D Dorian. Chromaticism occurs when you play from D♯ to E, for example – or from G♯ to A. D♯ is outside D Dorian, but resolves to E, which is part of the D Dorian scale; likewise, G♯ is outside D Dorian, but resolves to A, which is within D Dorian.

Chromaticism can also occur when resolving from one chord to another. In such a scenario, the stated tonality of the next chord in the sequence should serve as your primary consideration, to execute the strongest chromatic resolution.

For example, if the sequence of chords is Dm7 to G7 (ii7–V7, a half-cadence), you may choose to use Mixolydian (mode) when resolving to the G7. The stated tonality applied to the Dm7 is unimportant. For chromaticism to occur, you must play a note outside the stated tonality for G7, allowing it to act as a leading tone to resolve by a half step to a note within the stated tonality. For example, from G♯ to G or A, from A♯ to A or B, and so forth.

LEADING TONE

In Western music theory, the leading tone is understood as the seventh scale degree of the diatonic scale that leads melodically to the tonic of the home key. In the C major scale, for example, the leading tone is the note B; the leading tone chord is B-D-F, a diminished triad.

The leading tone resolves ("leads") to another note, one semitone higher. The leading tone also exists diatonically as the natural 3rd in the V chord and resolves up by a half step to the root of the I chord, for proper voice leading in an authentic cadence. Play the following etude, which features the leading tones for B♭ (A♮) and E♭ (D♮).

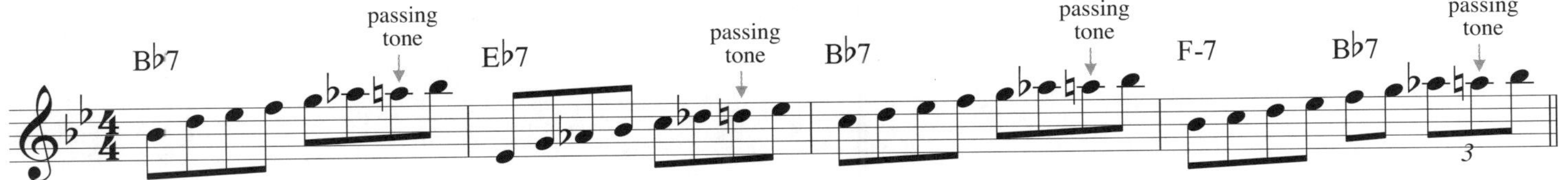

This exercise features leading tones resolving upward to the chord roots. Practice it on your instrument.

BEBOP SCALE

Bebop scales are derived from modes of the major, melodic minor, harmonic minor, and harmonic major scales. Bebop scales are created by adding a chromatic passing tone between whole steps in a diatonic seven-note scale, including all related modes. In jazz, the most commonly referenced bebop scales are Mixolydian and Dorian. Usually, Mixolydian bebop is referred to as the bebop scale and Dorian bebop is referred to as the minor bebop scale. Typically, bebop scales are thought of as containing a single chromatic passing tone between the ♭7th and the root, as shown below.

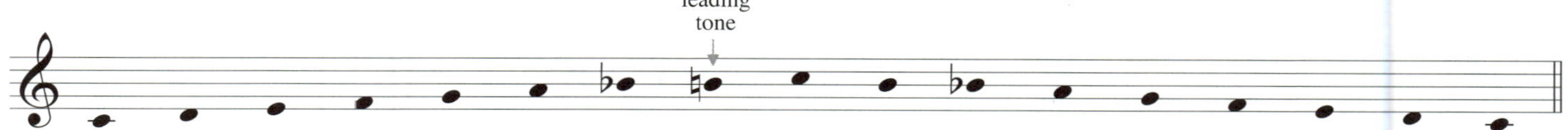

However, that configuration is only one of the possibilities for the myriad bebop scales. Each diatonic scale, for example, has five possible locations for the inserted chromatic passing tone. If applied to all four diatonic scale families (major, melodic minor, harmonic minor, harmonic major), each of the 28 modes has five possible bebop scale variations. This yields 140 bebop scales. C major, for example, contains seven modes:

- **C Ionian**
- **D Dorian**
- **E Phrygian**
- **F Lydian**
- **G Mixolydian**
- **A Aeolian**
- **B Locrian**

With the addition of a chromatic passing tone, each mode can become a bebop scale. The chromatic passing tone may occur between any whole step.

- **C Ionian bebop:** C-D-E-F-G-A-(A♯/B♭)-B
- **D Dorian bebop:** D-E-F-G-A-(A♯)-B-C
- **E Phrygian bebop:** E-F-G-A-(A♯/B♭)-B-C-D
- **F Lydian bebop:** F-G-A-A♯/B♭)-B-C-D-E)
- **G Mixolydian bebop:** G-A-(A♯/B♭)-B-C-D-E-F
- **A Aeolian bebop:** A-(A♯/B♭)-B-C-D-E-F-G
- **B Locrian bebop:** B-C-D-E-F-(F♯/G♭)-G-A

Bebop scales allow you to add chromaticism to improvisations in a linear fashion. Additionally, the chromatic passing tone, depending on both its placement and the use of swung eighth notes (or 16th notes, even), gives a variety of weak-beat/strong-beat emphasis. Bebop scales are usually played descending; however, learn these scales both ascending and descending, for technical fluency.

ENCLOSURE AND ENCLOSURES

Enclosure is a form of chromaticism in which a target note in the upcoming chord is preceded by, or enclosed by, other notes. Enclosure is used to emphasize or delay a particular resolution. The examples below show two-note enclosures; the target note is the third note in each case.

When creating an enclosure, the note immediately preceding the target note must be one half step away. Other notes in the enclosure can be a whole step away. An enclosure always ends with an approach a half step above or below the target note. Approximate enclosures are patterns used by jazz improvisers that appear to sound and function like enclosures, but which do not follow the rules of enclosure because notes approaching the target note are more than one half step away. Study the examples above.

Examples of three- and four-note enclosures are given below. In each case, the target note is the last one.

Three-Note Enclosures

Four-Note Enclosures

PLAYING EXERCISES

Practice each etude with a metronome, gradually increasing the tempo over a period of days and weeks. Work toward ♩ = 120.

Lower Leading Tone Study

Upper Leading Tone Study

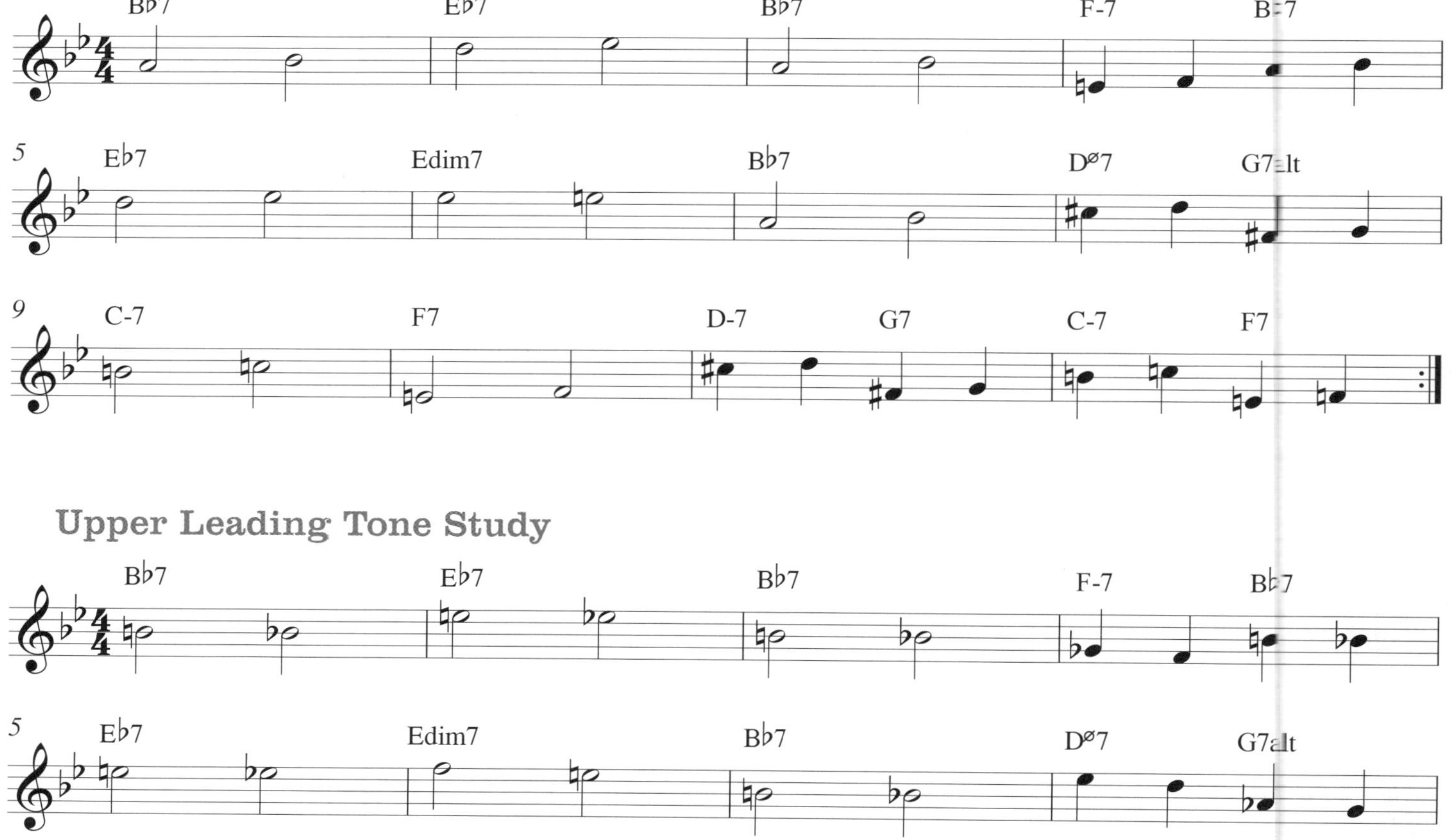

Leading Tone Study (Above and Below Chord Tones)

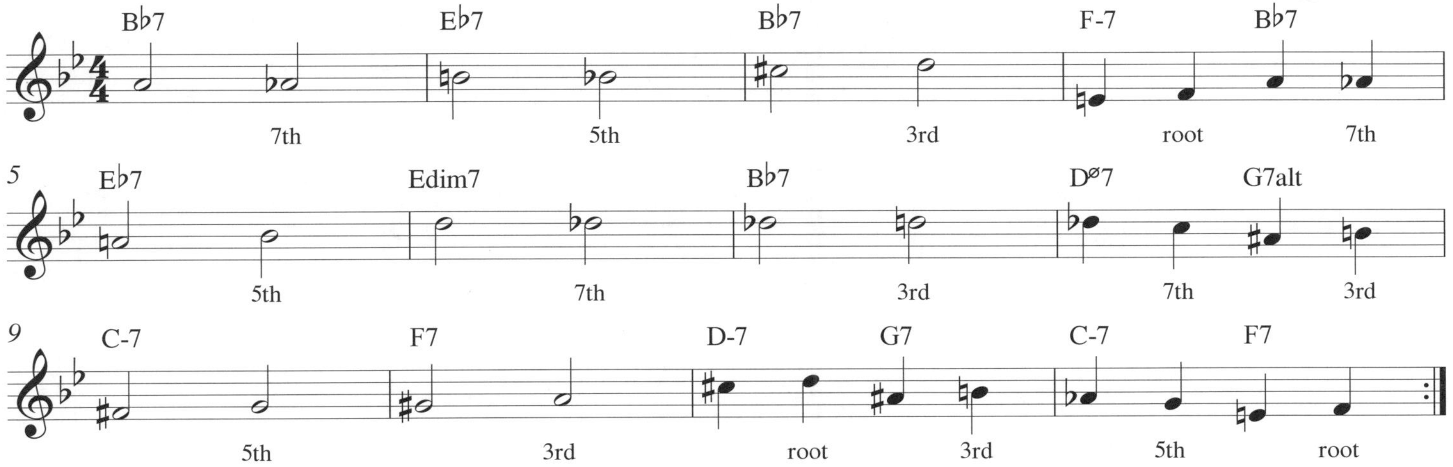

Leading Tone Study (Advanced)

Blues Bebop Scale Study #1 (V)

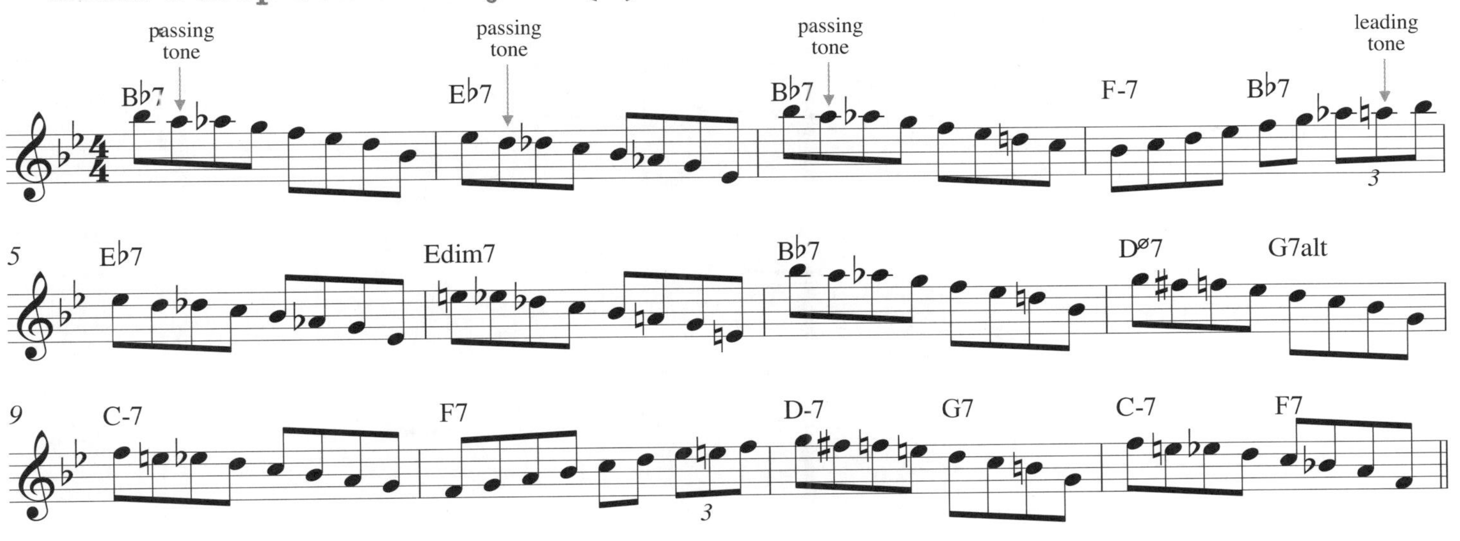

Blues Bebop Scale Study #1 (V, Retrograde)

Blues Bebop Scale Study #2 (IV)

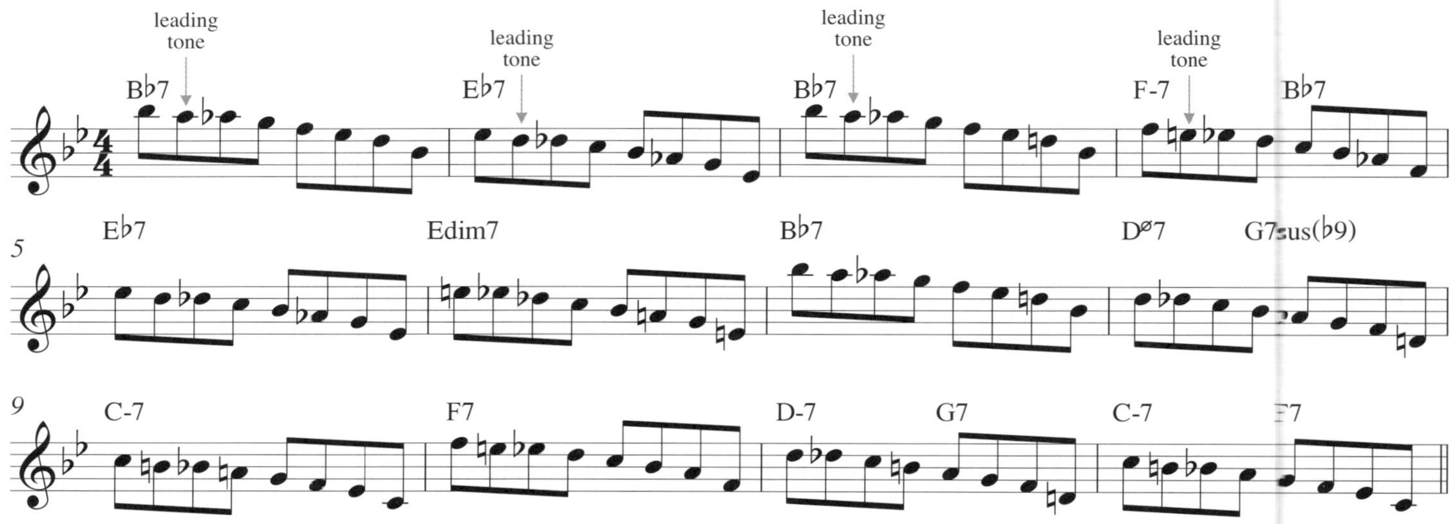

Blues Bebop Scale Study #2 (IV, Retrograde)

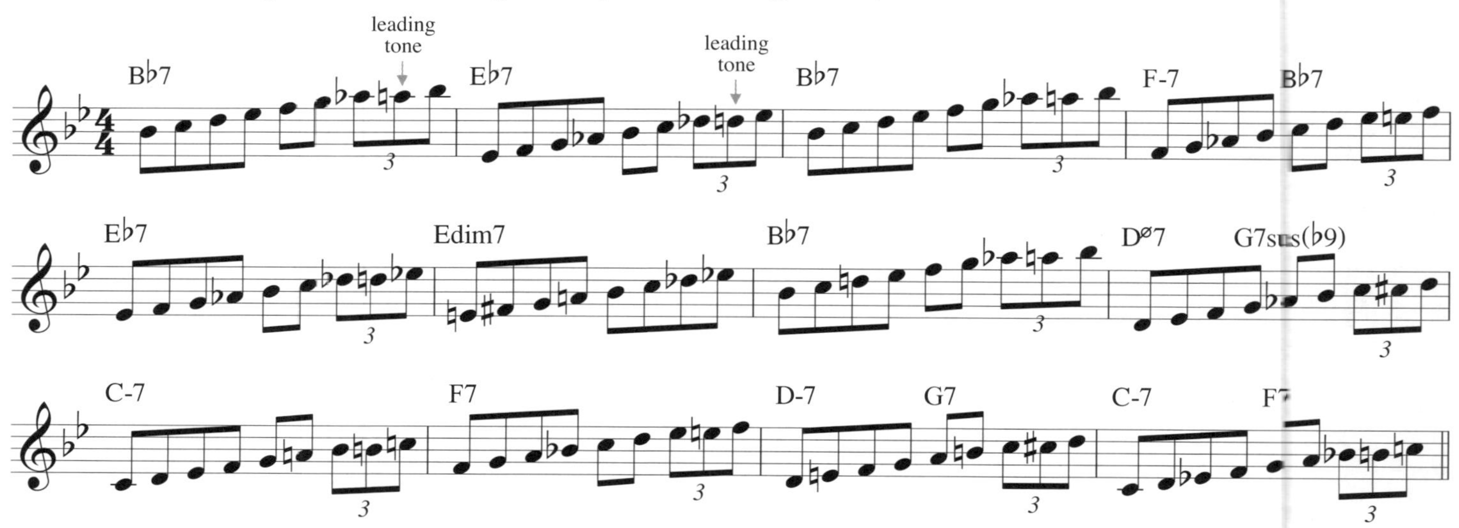

Continuous Bebop Scale Study (IV)

Blues Enclosure Study #1

Blues Enclosure Study #2

Blues Enclosure Study #3
B♭7
E♭7
3
B♭7
F-7
B♭7
5
E♭7
Edim7
7
B♭7
D∅7
G7sus(♭9)
9
C-7
F7
11
D-7
G7
C-7
F7
Blues Enclosure Study #4
B♭7
E♭7
3
B♭7
F-7
B♭7
5
E♭7
Edim7
7
B♭7
D∅7
G7sus(♭9)
9
C-7
F7
11
D-7
G7
C-7
F7

CHAPTER 8
PHRASING & ARTICULATION

Concepts, Scales, and Modes

- Phrasing and Articulation
- Metric Modulation
- Eighth-note Phrasing

In this chapter, we will concentrate on phrasing and articulation. You'll find a plethora of exercises that will help create phrases for improvisation. You'll learn to make intelligent choices regarding rhythm and phrasing. The concepts here will develop aural correlations with accenting and building rhythmic structures. **Remember:** Do not move on to other exercises until you have mastered each concept. You can do it!

EIGHTH-NOTE PHRASING

Eighth-note phrasing is particular to the emphasis of the note, on or off the beat. There are three basic types.

Prebop (1920s-1940s): Notes are swung with emphasis placed on the beat (the first part of the triplet).

Bebop (1940s-late 1950s): Notes are still swung, but emphasis is placed on the "and" of the beat (approximately the last eighth note of the triplet).

Postbop (1960s and beyond): Notes are almost even in value, with emphasis placed on the "and" of the beat; notes are played evenly.

GHOST NOTES

Ghost notes are notes that are de-emphasized, often to the point of near silence, within a musical phrase. These notes are sometimes referred to as "swallowed." In the example below, the ghost notes are shown as the letter ×.

ARTICULATION

Articulations are performance techniques that affect the duration of a note. There are many different styles of articulation (slurs, phrase marks, staccato, marcato accent, sforzandos, legato, etc.), each of which may be utilized for different effects. Articulations may also be varied and combined to create the phrasing idiomatic to the style of music performed and to bring clarity to the performer's phrasing. Additionally, articulations can be implemented in different ways to create rhythmic contrast – to affect the perception of tempo, meter, and of phrasing. Articulations play a key role in *phraseology*, communicating the fixed expressions, musical idioms, and stock phrases found in a music's genre.

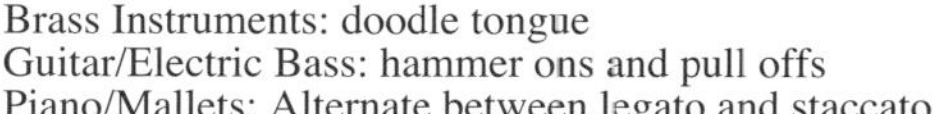

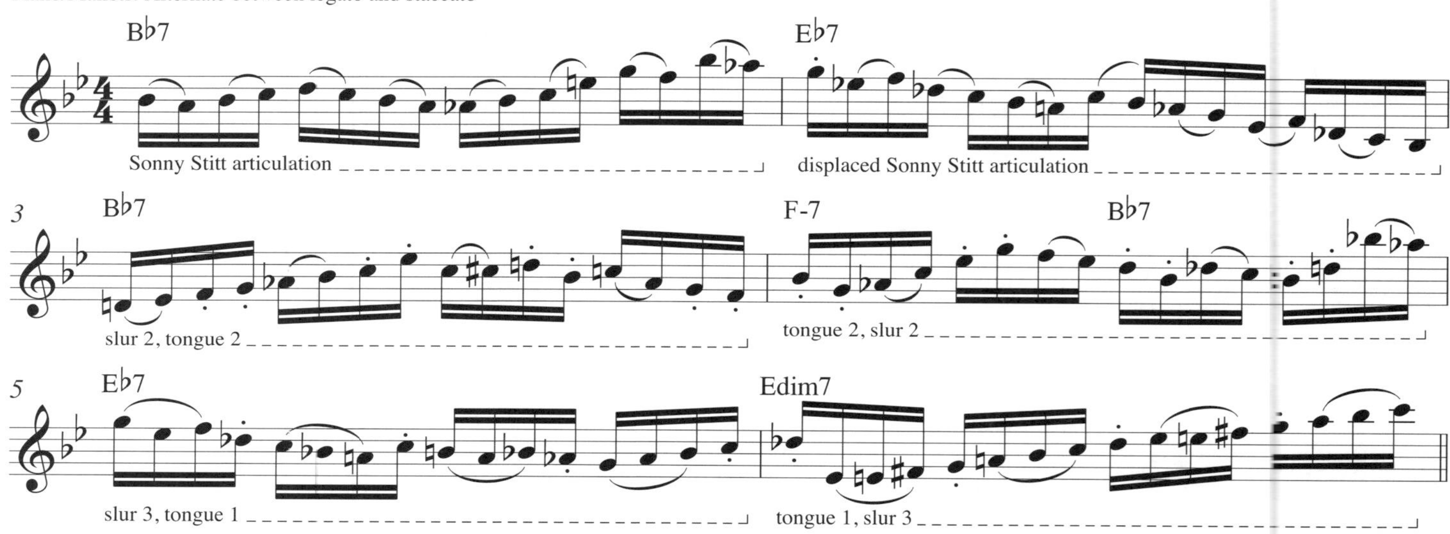

METRIC MODULATION

Phrasing

Phrasing plays a major role in the practice of *metric modulation*, which is to superimpose or aurally infer a different grouping of meter than is actually being played. For example, playing triplets in two-note or four-note groupings instead of three-note groupings implies compound time (2-over-3 or 3-over-4).

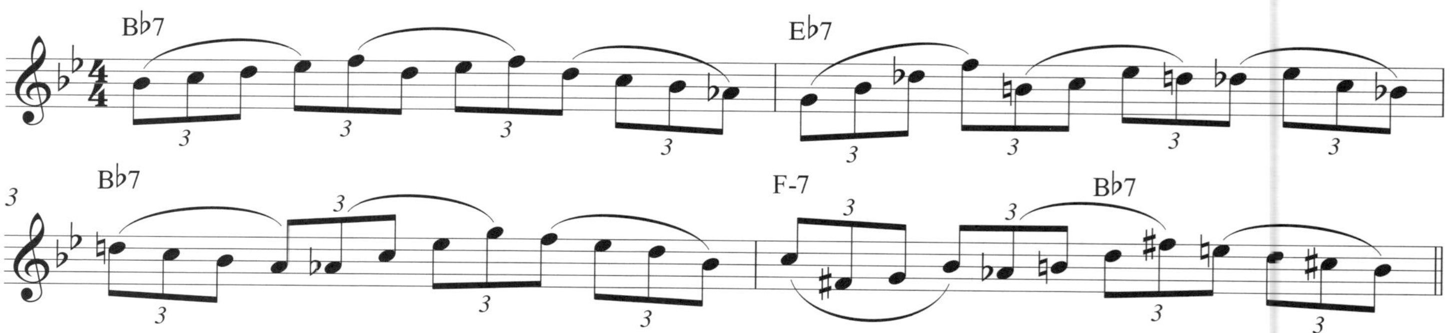

Metric modulation can change the perception of tempo and meter – to superimpose a different meter over the established meter and imply a change in tempo over the established pulse. The "new tempo" and original pulse can be linked either by a closely related or loosely related subdivision of the pulse.

Hemiola

Hemiola is another example of metric modulation. Hemiola can be heard when a group of notes displaces the beat in equal subdivisions, but is superimposed against the established meter (e.g., 4-over-3 or 3-over-4). In Western musical notation, a hemiola can occur both within and across established bar lines. In modern musical practice, when a repeated rhythmic pattern in simple triple time is articulated as if it were in simple duple time (e.g., 3/4 over 4/4), the result is a hemiola. Hemiola can also be applied to repeated rhythmic patterns that are contrary to the established pulse, causing the sensation of displacement. The following is an example of hemiola.

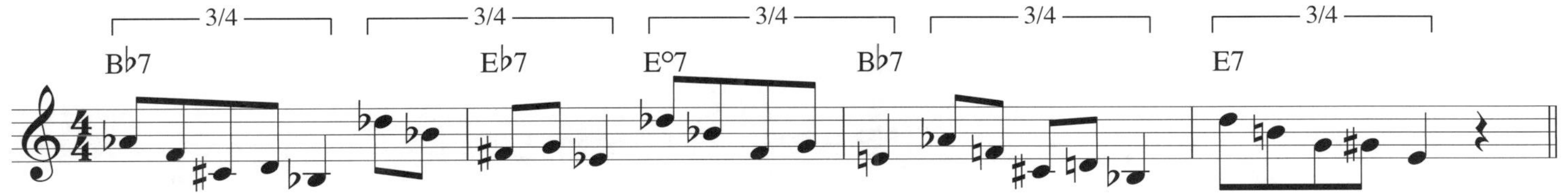

THE JOY OF TRIPLETS

You can add greater rhythmic contrast to improvisations by interspersing triplets – to break up the monotony of long eighth-note lines. Charlie Parker, for example, revolutionized the way triplets are used to create syncopation and define the beginning, middle, and end of a phrase. *Phraseology*, in this book, is the art of beginning and ending a line in a musically successful manner. (See page 143.)

Practice the following etude, which employs triplets in stepwise motion, chromatic passages, and arpeggios.

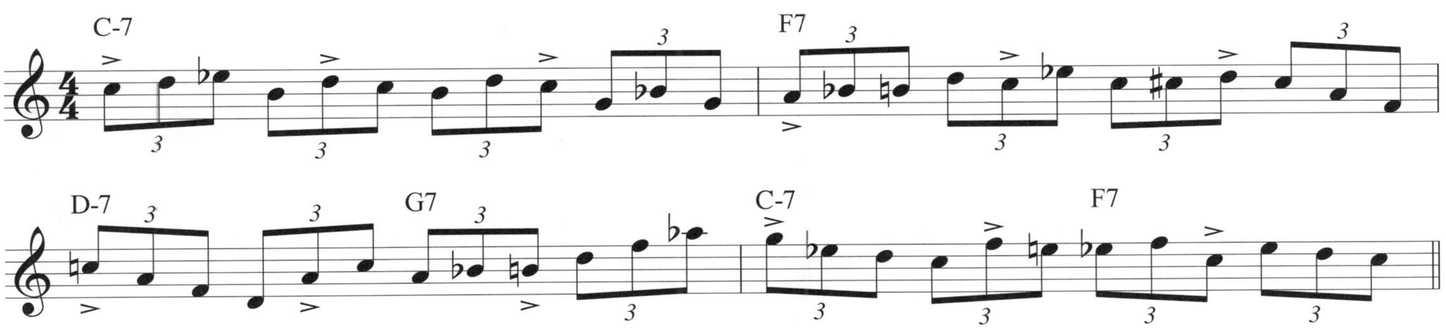

Now play this four-bar example, which intersperses triplets between eighth notes.

PLAYING EXERCISES

Practice each etude with a metronome, gradually increasing the tempo over a period of days and weeks. Work toward ♩ = 120.

Blues Articulation Study

This study features 12 different approaches to articulation. Play each articulation over the entire form, then mix and match to challenge yourself and add variety at the same time.

Blues Articulation Study Challenge

To use brass and woodwind parlance – in this etude, we slur three notes then tongue two notes. Transfer this articulation to your own particular instrument. Notice how the phraseology is affected here. Start slowly and increase the tempo over time.

Blues Rhythmic Eighth-Note Exercise

Blues Metric Modulation Exercise

Blues Eighth-Note Phrasing Exercise

CHAPTER 9
WHOLE-TONE & DIMINISHED SCALES

Concepts, Scales, and Modes

- Whole-Tone Scales
- Diminished Scales
- Inverted Diminished Scales

In this chapter, you will concentrate on whole-tone and diminished scales. There's a plethora of exercises to help you develop an ear for these scales and patterns as they relate to the blues progression. The concepts here will develop aural correlations with the sound of chords and with your technical facility to work inside and outside those structures. **Remember:** Do not move on to other exercises until you have mastered each concept. You can do it!

WHOLE-TONE SCALES

Whole-tone scales are hexatonic (six-note) scales in which each note is separated from its neighbors by one whole step. Enharmonic spelling of notes within whole-tone scales is standard practice. There are two unique whole-tone scales, with each scale having six modes. You should practice the modes of both whole-tone scales individually (i.e., treat them as 12 individual scales).

Whole-Tone Scales in C and D♭

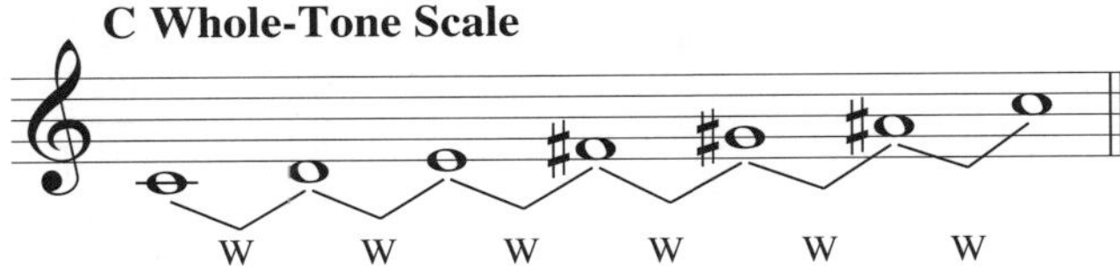

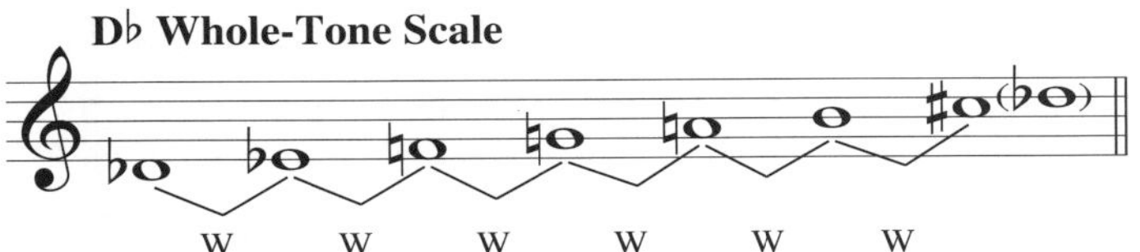

Whole-Tone Scales

(Enharmonic notes are in parentheses.)

Derived from C-D-E-F♯-G♯-A♯ whole-tone scale	**Derived from D♭-E♭-F-G-A-B whole-tone scale**
C-D-E-F♯-G♯-A♯	D♭-E♭-F-G-A-B
D-E-F♯-G♯-A♯-C	E♭-F-G-A-B-D♭
E-F♯-G♯-A♯-C-D	F-G-A-B-C♯(D♭)-D♯(E♭)
F♯-G♯-A♯-C-D-E	G-A-B-C♯(D♭)-D♯(E♭)-F
G♯-A♯-B♯(C)-D-E-F♯	A-B-C♯(D♭)-D♯(E♭)-F-G
A♯-B♯(C)-D-E-F♯-G♯	B-C♯(D♭)-D♯(E♭)-F-G-A

When playing the blues, whole-tone scales can be applied to any dominant 7th chord, as in the exercises that follow.

PLAYING EXERCISES (A)

Practice each etude with a metronome, gradually increasing the tempo over a period of days and weeks. Work toward ♩ = 120.

Blues Whole-Tone Scale Study – Ascending

implied chords: B♭9(♯11 ♯5) | E♭9(♯11 ♯5) | B♭9(♯11 ♯5) | B♭9(♯11 ♯5)
normal chords: B♭7 | E♭7 | B♭7 | F-7 B♭7

5
E♭9(♯11 ♯5) | E9(♯11 ♯5) | B♭9(♯11 ♯5) | G9(♯11 ♯5)
E♭7 | Edim7 | B♭7 | D∅7 G7alt

9
F9(♯11 ♯5) | F9(♯11 ♯5) | G9(♯11 ♯5) | F9(♯11 ♯5)
C-7 | F7 | D-7 G7 | C-7 F7

Blues Whole-Tone Scale Study – Descending

implied chords: B♭9(♯11 ♯5) | E♭9(♯11 ♯5) | B♭9(♯11 ♯5) | B♭9(♯11 ♯5)
normal chords: B♭7 | E♭7 | B♭7 | F-7 B♭7

5
E♭9(♯11 ♯5) | E9(♯11 ♯5) | B♭9(♯11 ♯5) | G9(♯11 ♯5)
E♭7 | Edim7 | B♭7 | D∅7 G7alt

9
F9(♯11 ♯5) | F9(♯11 ♯5) | G9(♯11 ♯5) | F9(♯11 ♯5)
C-7 | F7 | D-7 G7 | C-7 F7

Blues Whole-Tone Scale Study – Alternating (A)

Blues Whole-Tone Scale Study – Alternating (B)

Blues Whole-Tone Scale Study #1 – Root Relationship

motif

implied chords:
normal chords:

B♭9(♯11 ♯5) B♭7 — root

E♭9(♯11 ♯5) E♭7 — root

B♭9(♯11 ♯5) B♭7 — root

B♭9(♯11 ♯5) F-7 B♭7 — *pattern continues*

5

E♭9(♯11 ♯5) E♭7 — root

E9(♯11 ♯5) Edim7 — root

B♭9(♯11 ♯5) B♭7 — root

G9(♯11 ♯5) Dø7 G7alt — root

9

F9(♯11 ♯5) C-7 — root

F9(♯11 ♯5) F7 — *pattern continues*

G9(♯11 ♯5) D-7 G7 — root

F9(♯11 ♯5) C-7 F7 — root

Blues Whole-Tone Scale Study #2 – Half-Step Relationship

Blues Whole-Tone Scale Study #3 – Stepwise Relationship

DIMINISHED SCALES

Diminished scales are octatonic (eight-note) scales patterned in sequential whole steps and half steps. There are two types of diminished scales: diminished and inverted diminished. Diminished scales begin the whole-step/half step pattern with a whole step.

Diminished Scales (starting with a whole step)

Practice the modes of each diminished scale individually, treating them as 24 individual scales (12 for diminished, 12 for inverted diminished).

Modes of Diminished Scales

C-E♭-G♭-A (diminished)	**D♭-E-G-B♭ (diminished)**	**D-F-A♭-B (diminished)**
C-D-E♭-F-G♭-A♭-A-B	D♭-E♭-E-G♭-G-A-B♭-C	D-E-F-G-A♭-A-B-C-D♭
E♭-F-G♭-A♭-A-B-C-D	E-F♯-G-A-B♭-C-D♭-E♭	F-G-A♭-B♭-B-C♯-D-E
G♭-A♭-A-B-C-D-E♭-F	G-A-B♭-C-D♭-E♭-E-F♯	A♭-B♭-C♭-D♭-D-E-F-G
A-B-C-D-E♭-F-G♭-A♭	B♭-C-D♭-E♭-E-F♯-G-A	B-C♯-D-E-F-G-A♭-B♭

A diminished scale can be applied to any kind of minor chord, minor 7th chord (-7 or -7♭5), half-diminished 7th chord (ø7), or fully-diminished 7th chord (dim7).

INVERTED DIMINISHED SCALES

Inverted diminished scales, also known as half-whole diminished, begin with a half step.

Inverted Diminished Scales (starting with a half step)

Practice the modes of each diminished scale individually, treating them as 24 individual scales (12 for diminished, 12 for inverted diminished).

Modes of Inverted Diminished Scales

C-E♭-F♯(G♭)-A (inverted diminished)	D♭-E-G-B♭ (inverted diminished)	D-F-A♭-B (inverted diminished)
C-D♭-E♭-E-F♯-G-A-B♭	D♭-D-E-F-G-A♭-B♭-B	D-E♭-F-G♭-A♭-A-B-C♯
E♭-E-F♯-G-A-B♭-C-D♭	E-F-G-A♭-B♭-B-C♯-D	F-G♭-A♭-A-B-C♯-D-E♭
F♯-G-A-B♭-C-D♭-E♭-E	G-A♭-B♭-B-C♯-D-E-F	A♭-A-B-C♯-D-E♭-F-G♭
A-B♭-C-D♭-E♭-E-F♯-G	B♭-B-C♯-D-E-F-G-A♭	B-C♯-D-E♭-F-G♭-A♭-A

An inverted diminished scale can be applied to any kind of dominant chord. Diminished scales may also be applied to chords in a manner more specific to the type of chord available. The chart below lists several options.

Possible Scales for Half-Diminished 7th Chords

ø7 or -7(♭5)	-7(♯11) *	Minor Lydian/Mixolydian (4th mode of harmonic minor)
	-7(♭13, ♭9, ♭5)*	Locrian (7th mode of major)
	-7(♭13, ♭5)*	Diminished/Whole Tone (6th mode of melodic minor)
	-7(♭9)**	Dorian ♭2 (2nd mode of melodic minor)
	-7(♭9, ♭5)**	Half-Diminished (2nd mode of harmonic minor)
	-7(♭5)**	Dorian ♭5 (2nd mode of harmonic major)

* - Generic treatments for subdominant with any type of altered dominant chord.
** - Determined by the altered dominant chord especially when tonicizing the I chord.

PLAYING EXERCISES (B)

Practice each etude with a metronome, gradually increasing the tempo over a period of days and weeks. Work toward ♩ = 120.

Blues Diminished Scale Study – Ascending

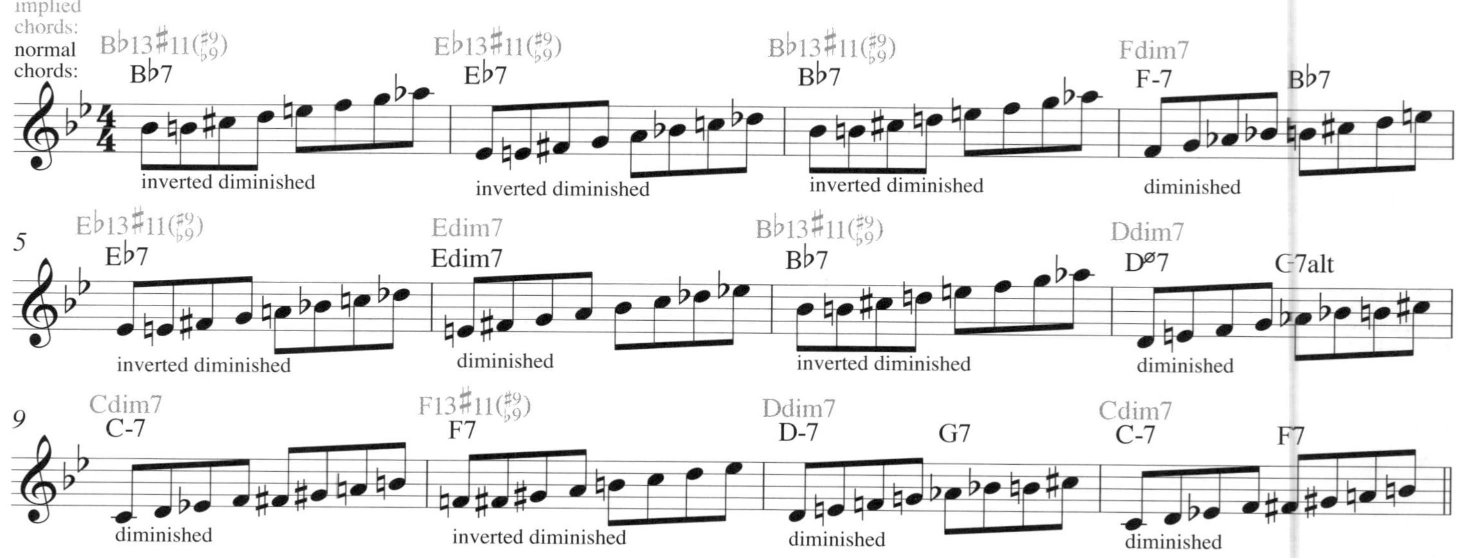

Blues Diminished Scale Study – Descending

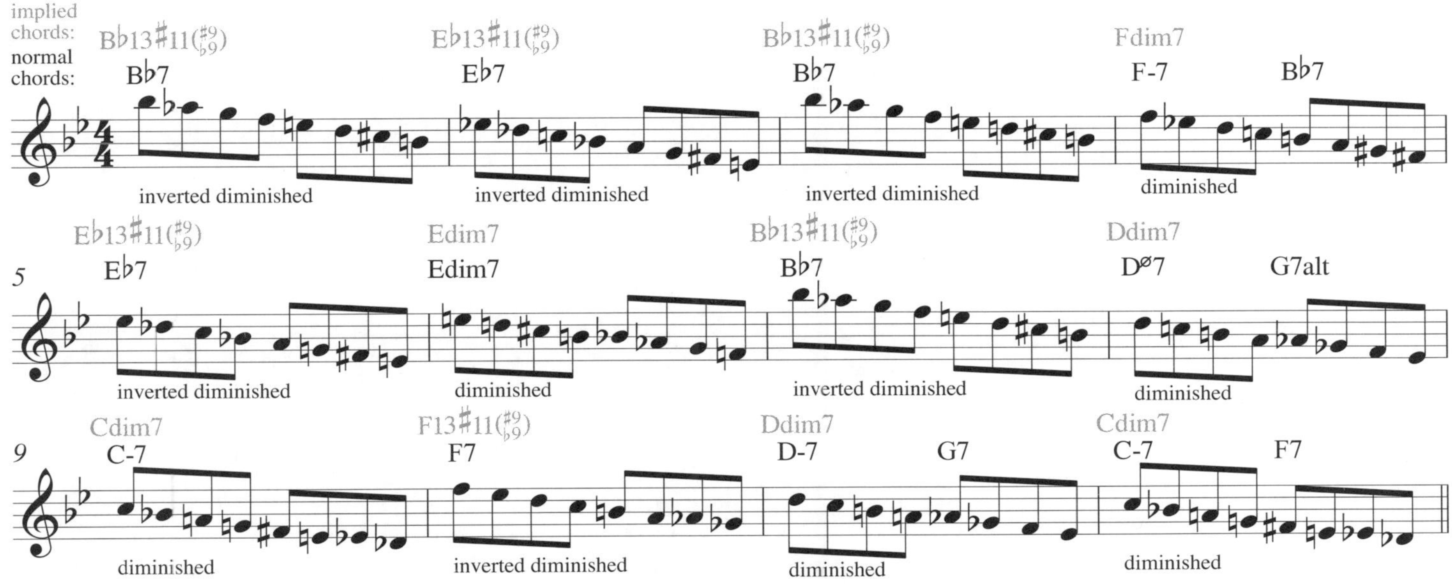

Blues Diminished Scale Study – Alternating (A)

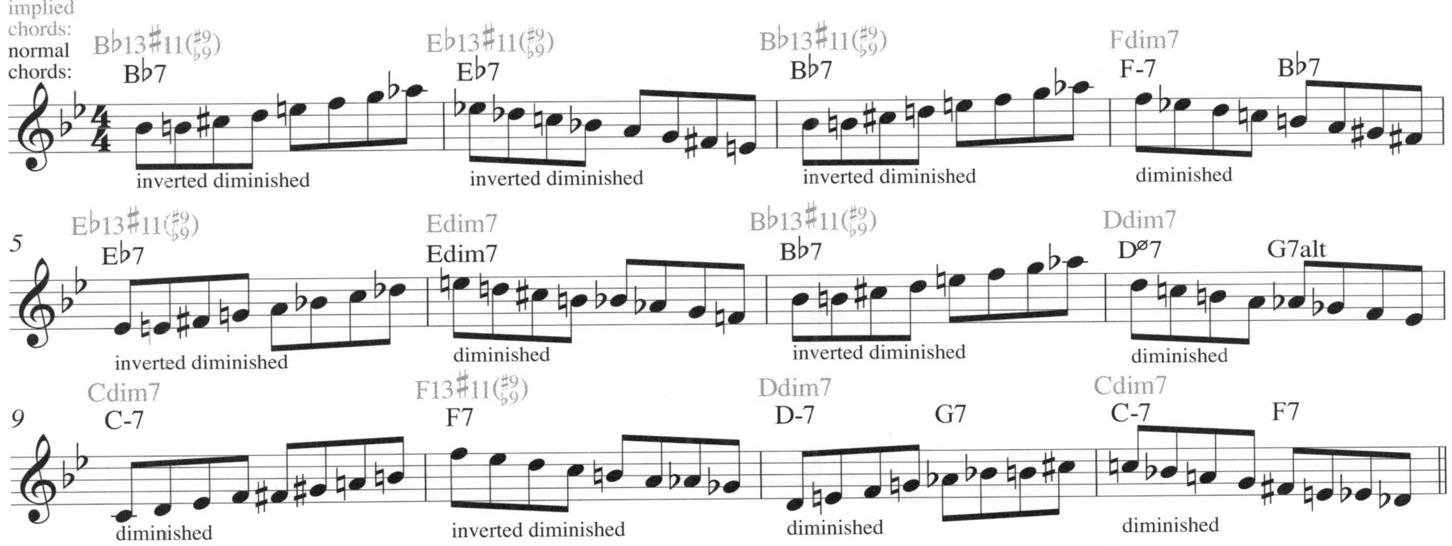

Blues Diminished Scale Study – Alternating (B)

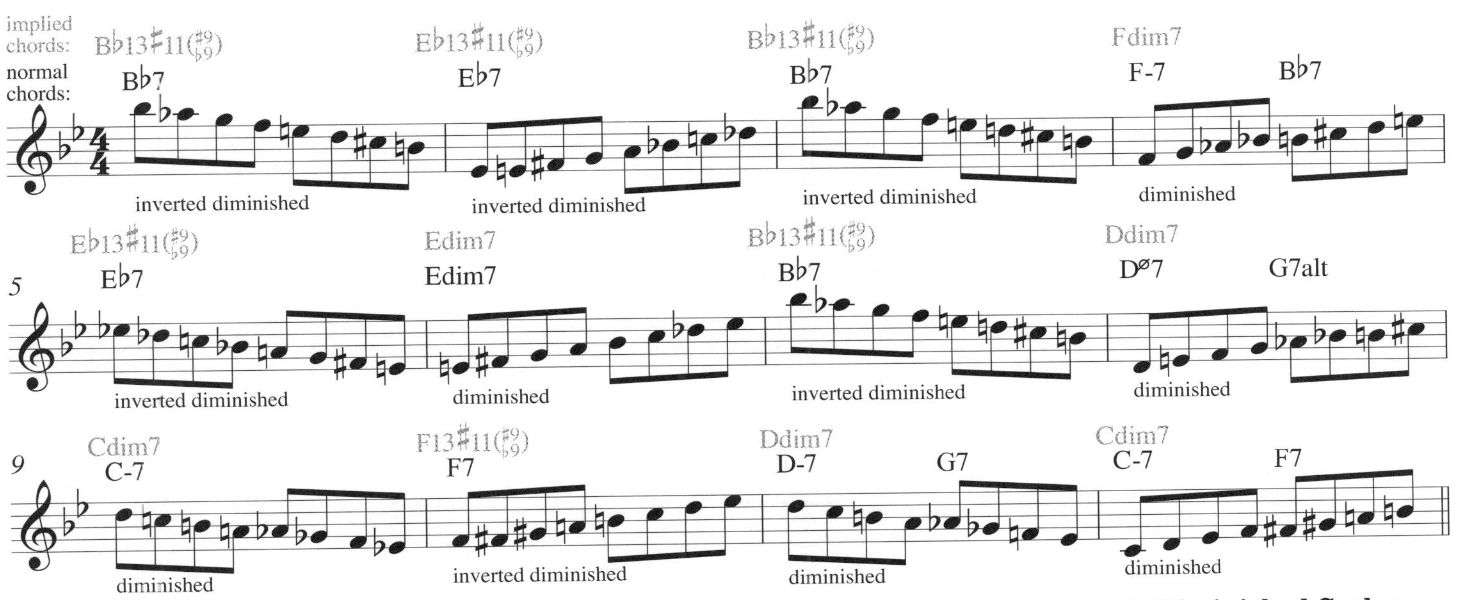

Blues Diminished Pattern Study #1 – Root Relationship
Motif
Motif (up perfect 4th)
Motif (up major 3rd)
implied chords:
normal chords:
Bb13#11(#9 b9)
Bb7
inverted diminished (starts on root)
Eb13#11(#9 b9)
Eb7
inverted diminished (starts on root)
Bb13#11(#9 b9)
Bb7
inverted diminished (starts on root)
Fdim7
F-7
Bb7
diminished (starts on 9)
5
Eb13#11(#9 b9)
Eb7
inverted diminished (starts on root)
Edim7
Edim7
diminished (starts on 9)
Bb13#11(#9 b9)
Bb7
inverted diminished (starts on root)
Ddim7
Dø7
G7alt
diminished (starts on 9)
9
Cdim7
C-7
diminished (starts on 9)
F13#11(#9 b9)
F7
inverted diminished (starts on root)
Ddim7
D-7
G7
diminished (starts on 9)
Cdim7
C-7
F7
diminished (starts on 9)
Blues Diminished Pattern Study #2 – Half-Step Relationship
motif
motif (up half step)
motif (down half step)
implied chords:
normal chords:
Bb13#11(#9 b9)
Bb7
inverted diminished motif
Eb13#11(#9 b9)
Eb7
inverted diminished motif (down half step)
Bb13#11(#9 b9)
Bb7
inverted diminished motif
Fdim7
F-7
Eb7
(diminished)
pattern continues

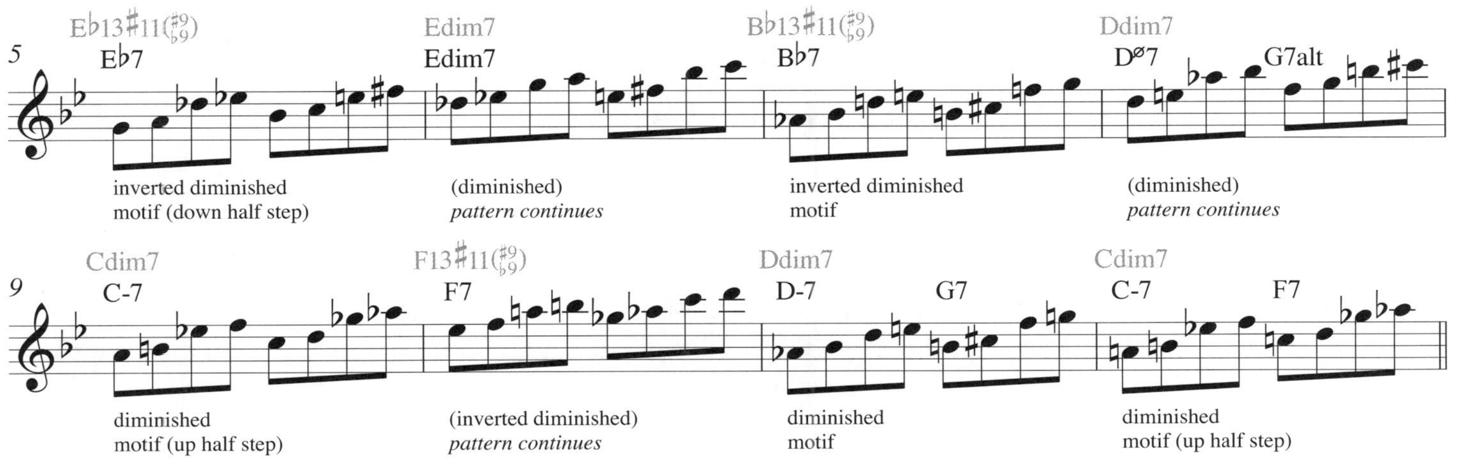

Blues Diminished Pattern Study #3 – Stepwise Relationship

motif

motif (up half step)

motif (down half step)

implied chords: B♭13♯11(♯9 ♭9) E♭13♯11(♯9 ♭9) B♭13♯11(♯9 ♭9) Fdim7

normal chords: B♭7 E♭7 B♭7 F-7 B♭7

inverted diminished motif | inverted diminished motif (down half step) | inverted diminished motif | (diminished) *pattern continues*

5 E♭13♯11(♯9 ♭9) Edim7 B♭13♯11(♯9 ♭9) Ddim7

E♭7 Edim7 B♭7 Dø7 G7alt

inverted diminished motif (down half step) | (diminished) *pattern continues* | inverted diminished motif | (diminished) *pattern continues*

9 Cdim7 F13♯11(♯9 ♭9) Ddim7 Cdim7

C-7 F7 D-7 G7 C-7 F7

diminished motif (up half step) | (inverted diminished) *pattern continues* | diminished motif | diminished motif (up half step)

CHAPTER 10
AUGMENTED SCALES

Concepts, Scales, and Modes

- Augmented Scales
- Inverted Augmented Scales

In this chapter, you will concentrate on augmented scales. There are lots of exercises to help you get familiar with some of the possible chord-scale relationships regarding augmented and inverted augmented scales. The concepts here will develop aural correlations with the sound of chords, as well as your technical facility to work inside and outside of those structures. **Remember:** Do not move on to other exercises until you have mastered each concept. You can do it!

AUGMENTED SCALES

The augmented scale, also known as the symmetrical augmented scale, is constructed of two augmented triads a minor 3rd apart – e.g., C-E-G♯ and E♭-G-B). Enharmonic spelling of notes within augmented scales is common practice.

There are three unique augmented scales – each scale having four modes. Practice each mode of the augmented scale individually, treating them as 12 individual scales for augmented and 12 individual scales for inverted augmented.

Augmented Scales – beginning with an augmented 2nd (enharmonic minor 3rd)

Modes of the Augmented Scale – augmented 2nd (enharmonic minor 3rd)

C-E♭-G♭-A augmented	**D♭-E-G-B♭ augmented**	**D-F-A♭-B augmented**
C-D♯-E-G-A♭-B	D♭-E-F-A♭-A-C	D-E♯-F♯-A-B♭-C♯
E♭-F♯-G-B♭-C♭-D	E-F𝄪-G♯-B-C-D♯	F-G♯-A-C-D♭-E
G♭-A-B♭-D♭-E𝄫-F	G-A♯-B-D-E♭-F♯	A♭-B-C-E♭-F♭-G
A-B♯-C♯-E-F-G♯	B♭-C♯-D-F-G♭-A	B-C𝄪-D♯-F♯-G♭-A

The augmented scale can be applied to any kind of minor 7th or half-diminished 7th chord.

INVERTED AUGMENTED SCALES

Inverted augmented scales begin their pattern with a half step. They are constructed of two augmented triads placed one half step apart from another – e.g., C-E-G♯ and D♭-F-A. Enharmonic spelling of notes within inverted augmented scales is common practice.

There are three unique inverted augmented scales – each scale having four modes. Practice each mode of the augmented scale individually (i.e., treat them as 12 individual scales for augmented and 12 individual scales for inverted augmented).

Inverted Augmented Scales – beginning with half step

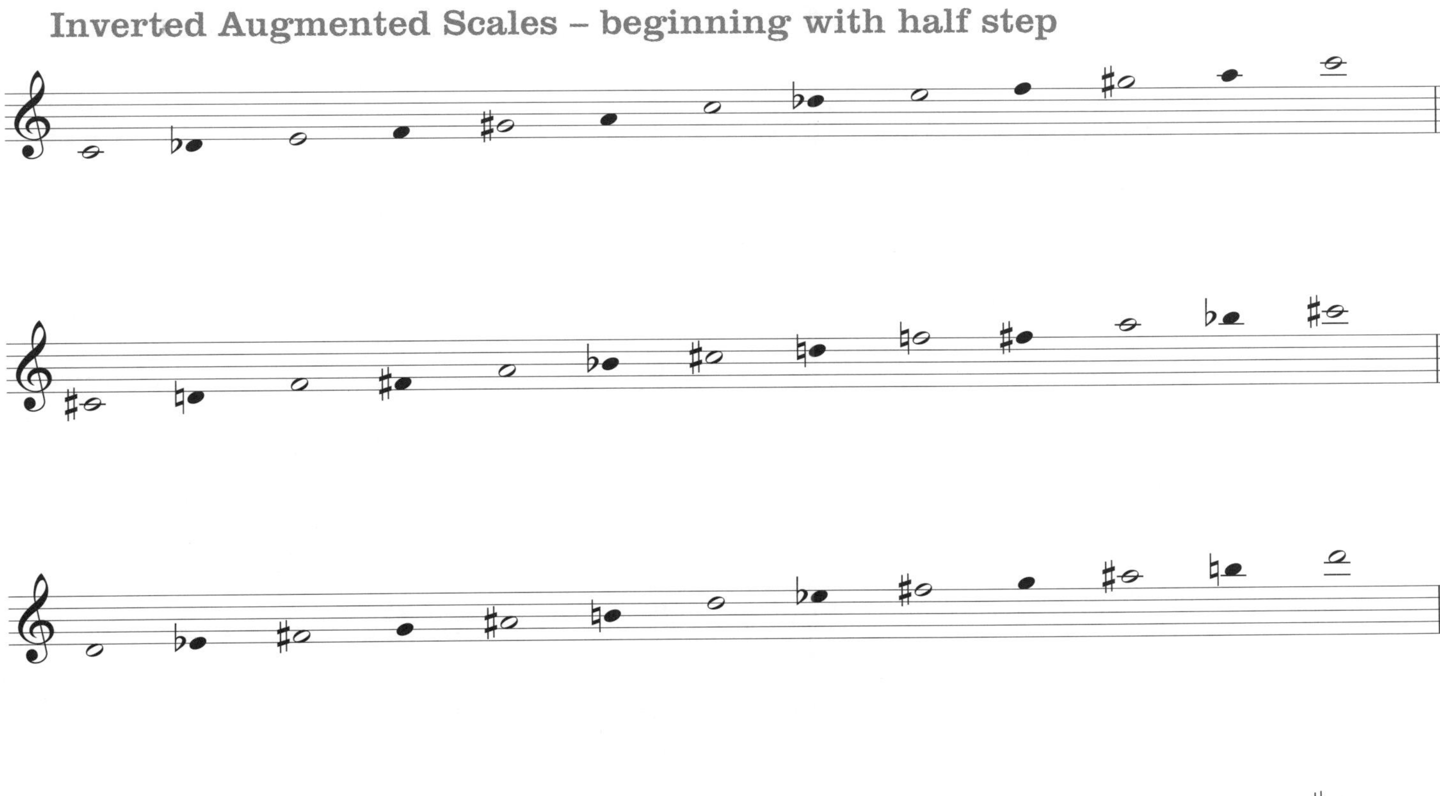

Modes of the Inverted Augmented Scale (half step)

C-E♭-G♭-A augmented	D♭-E-G-B♭ augmented	D-F-A♭-B augmented
C-D♭-E-F-G♯-A	D♭-E♭♭-F-G♭-A-B♭	D-E♭-F♯-G-A♯-B
E♭-F♭♭-G-A♭-C♭-C	E-F-G♯-A-C-D♭	F-G♭-A-B♭-D♭-D
G♭-G-B♭-B-D♭-D	G-A♭-C♭-C-E♭-E	A♭-A-C-E♭-E-G♭
A-B♭-D♭-D-F-G♭	B♭-B-D-E♭-G♭-G	B-C-E♭-E-G♭-G

The inverted augmented scale can be applied to any kind of dominant chord (for example, V7 or V7alt). Augmented scales may also be used to tonicize a minor I chord. Additionally, they can be employed as substitutions for configurations of the harmonic minor scale. These possibilities will be explored in Chapter 12.

Harmonic Minor Substitutions using Augmented and Inverted Augmented Scales

Augmented	harmonic minor (mode 1)
Inverted augmented	major/augmented (mode 3)
Inverted augmented	augmented Phrygian (mode 5)
Augmented	Lydian "split 3rd" (mode 6)
Inverted augmented	altered ♭6 (mode 7)

PLAYING EXERCISES

Practice each etude with a metronome, gradually increasing the tempo over a period of days and weeks. Work toward ♩ = 120.

Blues Augmented Scale Study – Ascending

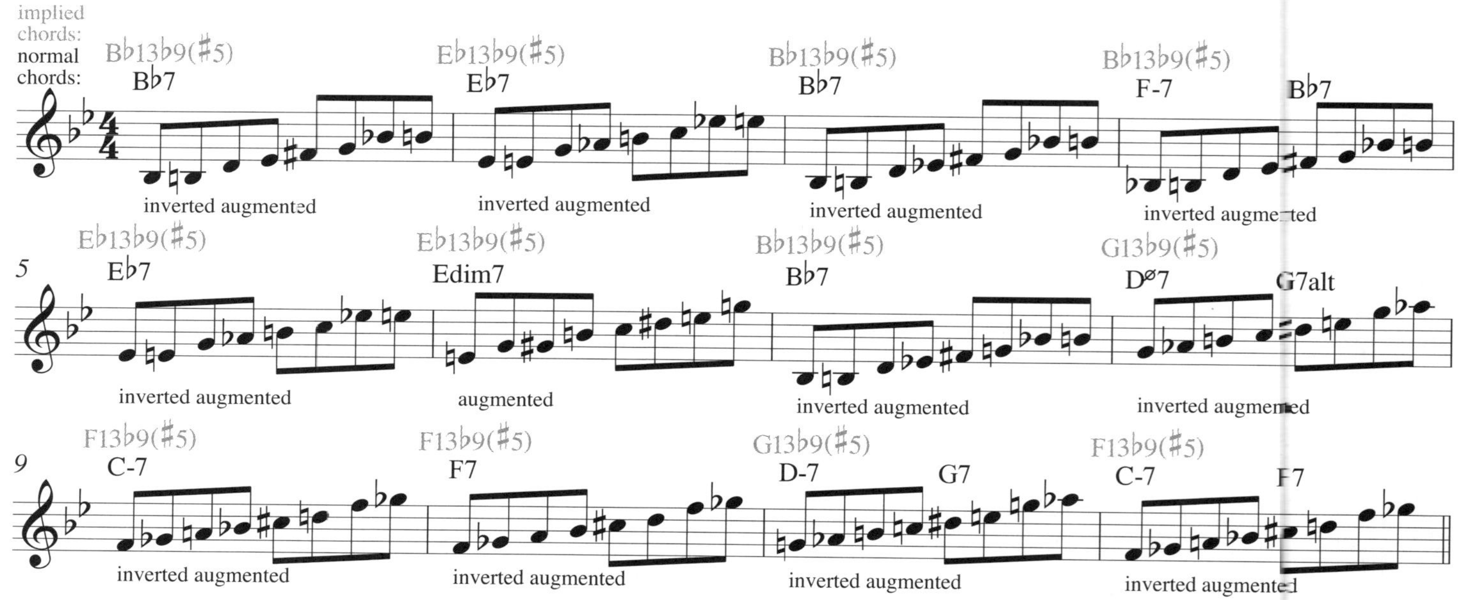

Blues Augmented Scale Study – Descending

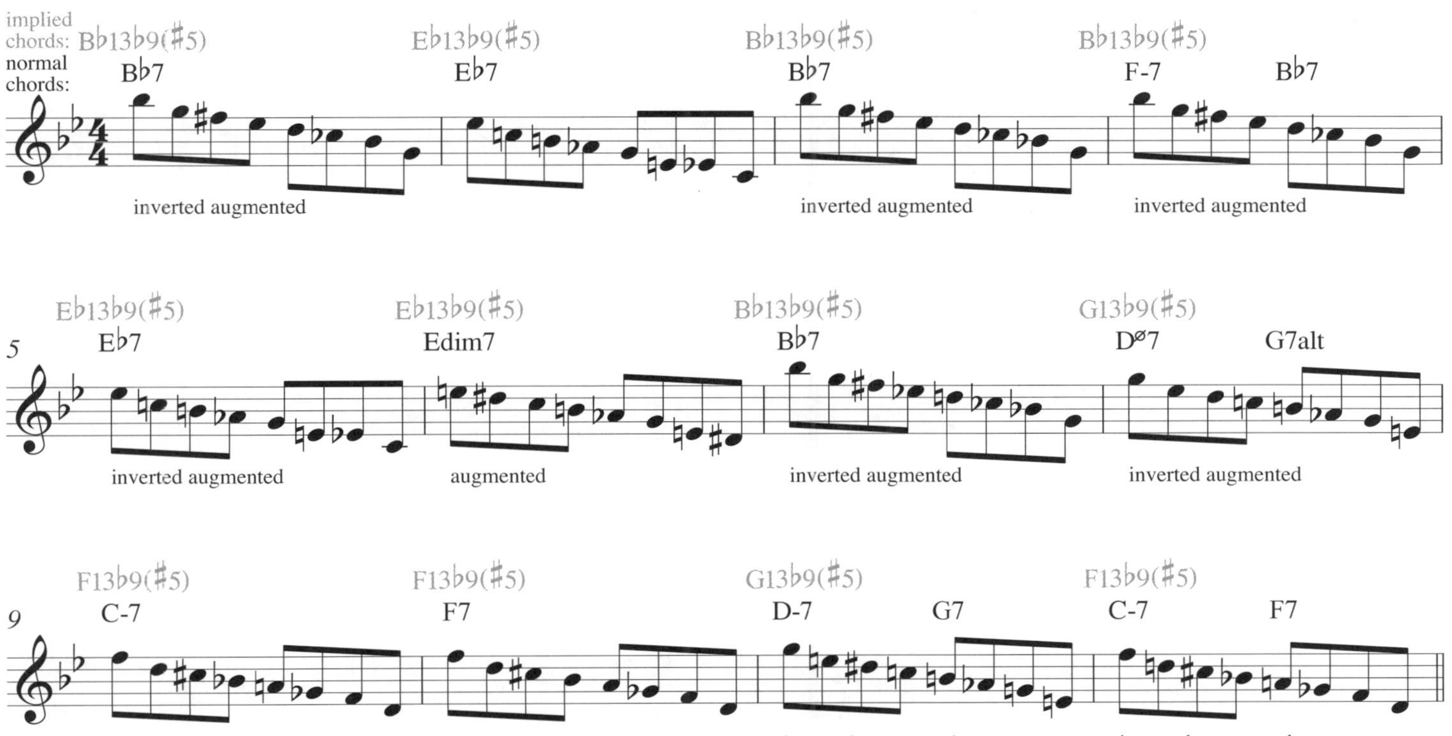

Blues Augmented Scale Study – Alternating (A)

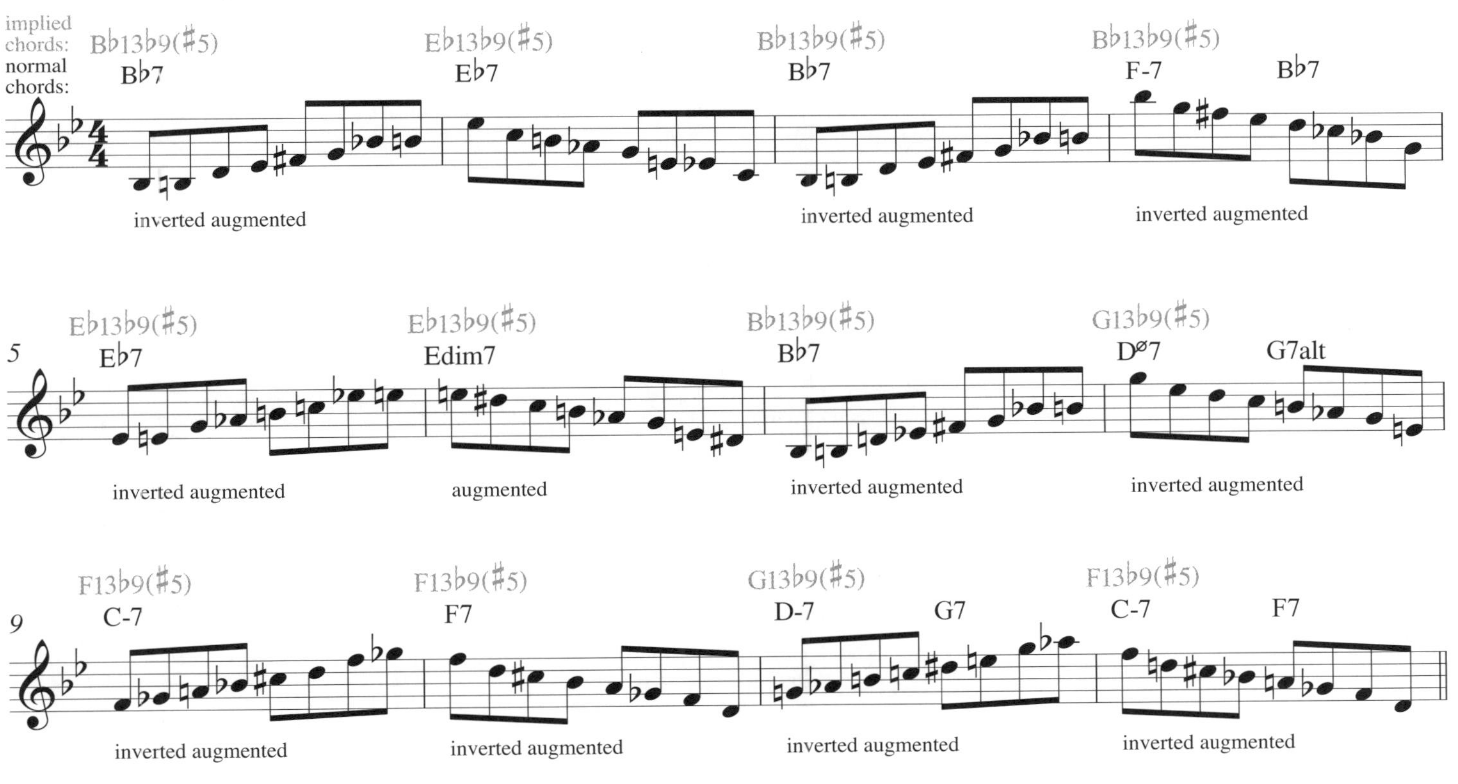

Blues Augmented Scale Study – Alternating (B)

Blues Augmented Pattern Study #1 – Root Relationship

Blues Augmented Pattern Study #2 – Half-/Whole-Step Relationship

motif
motif (down half step)

motif (down whole step)
motif (up half step)

B♭7 E♭7 B♭7 F-7 B♭7

motif
motif (up half step)
motif
pattern continues

5 E♭7 Edim7 B♭7 Dø7 G7sus(♭9)

motif (up half step)
pattern continues
motif
motif (up half step)

9 C-7 F7 D-7 G7 C-7 F7

motif (down half step)
pattern continues
motif (up half step)
motif (down half step)

Blues Augmented Pattern Study #3 – Stepwise Relationship

motif
motif (up minor 2nd)

motif (up minor 3rd)
motif (up major 2nd)

B♭7 E♭7 B♭7 F-7 B♭7

moving up
moving down
moving up
moving down

motif
motif (up half step)
motif
pattern continues

5 E♭7 Edim7 B♭7 Dø7 G7sus(♭9)

moving up
moving down
moving up

motif (up half step)
pattern continues
motif
motif (up half step)

9 C-7 F7 D-7 G7 C-7 F7

moving down
moving up
moving down
moving up

motif (up half step)
pattern continues
motif (up half step)
motif (up half step)

GOING FORWARD

Here are a few reminders about…

…Patterns and Relationships

The goals of the exercises in the chapter are to provide you with a firm foundation in harmony, facilitate the creation of patterns from any note, and to connect the patterns using the most efficient means possible.

…Root Relationships

Building patterns from the root allows you to explore the sound of each chord from the foundation of the harmony.

…Half-Step Relationships

Building patterns from half-step relationships frees you from having to start or continue a pattern from the root of the chord. You are emancipated from the bias inherent to root relationships and can now maximize the amount of material that can be played in a specific range. You can connect patterns using the smallest interval available.

…Stepwise Relationships

Stepwise relationships are an expansion of half-step relationships – connecting structures by half steps or whole steps as needed to facilitate the connection of patterns using smaller intervals. It is similar to the concept of continuous scales in that you are restricted to specific intervals (half steps and whole steps); it also provides another escape from root bias by restricting the next pattern to a whole step or half step away.

CHAPTER 11
BIRD BLUES & HARMONIC MAJOR

Concepts, Scales & Modes

- Bird Blues
- Harmonic Major Scale

In this chapter, we'll learn about Bird Blues and the harmonic major scale. The concepts here will develop aural correlations with the sounds of these, and will increase your technical facility to work inside and outside of them. **Remember:** Do not move on to other exercises until you have mastered each concept. You can do it!

BIRD BLUES

A Bird Blues is a variation of the 12-bar jazz blues in which the structure of the tune "Confirmation," written by Charlie "Bird" Parker, is superimposed over the 12-bar jazz blues form. Although "Confirmation" and the Bird Blues differ in overall structure, they are similar in that descending ii–V patterns are used to transition smoothly from key center to key center in four-bar increments.

Bird Blues in F

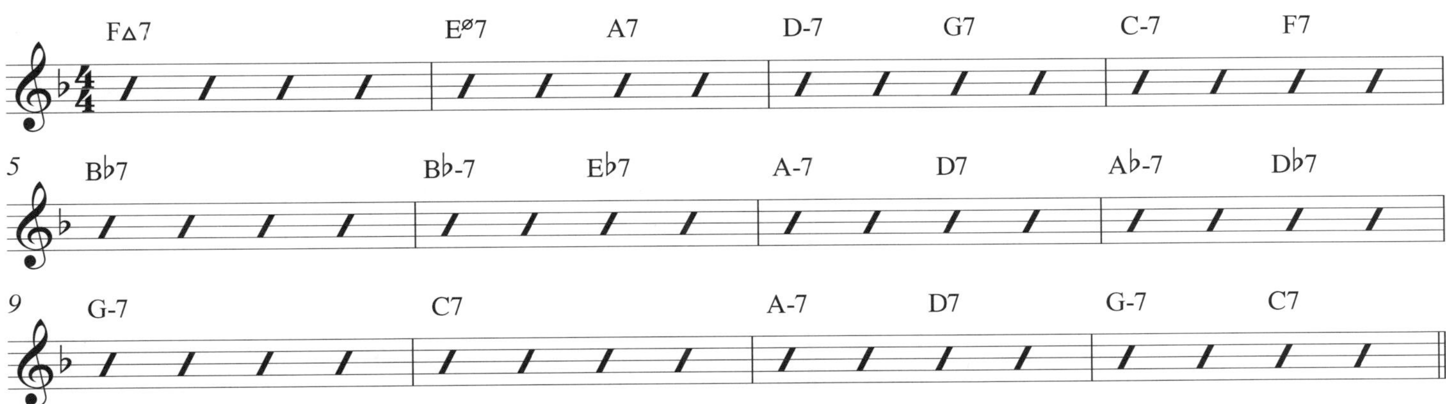

In a Bird Blues, ii–V patterns descending in whole steps connect the key center in bar 1 to the key center in bar 5. The ii–V progression descending in half steps connects the key center in bar 5 to the key center in bar 9. The last four bars of the Bird Blues are identical to the structure in the jazz blues. The chords in first five bars of a Bird Blues progression are identical to those used in "Confirmation," providing another indication of the close relationship between "Confirmation" and Bird Blues.

Bird Blues in F, with patterns

HARMONIC MAJOR SCALE

The harmonic major scale is a major scale with lowered 6th (♭13). It offers a canvas approach to an altered ii–V pattern that resolves to a major I in which the harmonic function of the progression supersedes the dissonance produced by the lowered 6th (♭13).

C Harmonic Major

CΔ11♭13
CΔ7♭13
CΔ7♭13

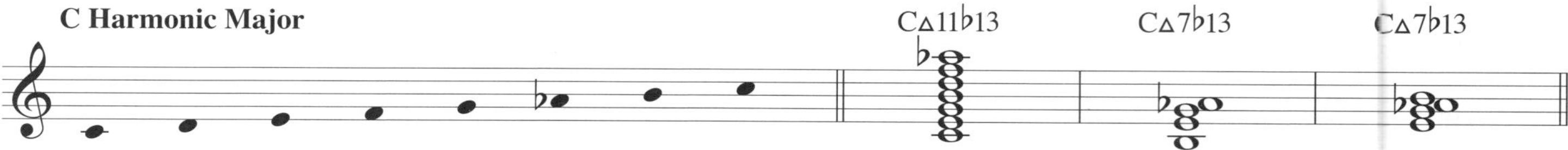

In a standard ii–V–I progression, in which the chords receive no alterations, you can use a scale built from the I chord to address all the notes in a ii–V–I (e.g., Gm7–C7–Fmaj7 = F major scale). In an altered ii7♭5–V7♭9 that resolves to a major I, a harmonic major scale built from the I chord can be used to address all the notes in the chord progression (e.g., Gm7♭5–C7♭9–Fmaj7 = F harmonic major scale).

Harmonic Major Modes Diatonic

C Harmonic Major

CΔ11♭13
CΔ7♭13
CΔ7♭13

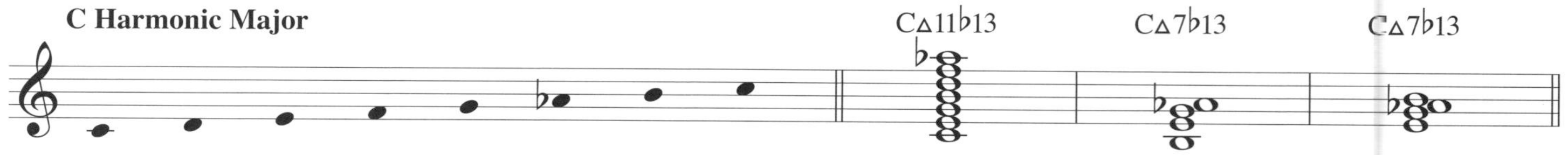

D Dorian ♭5

D-13♭5
D-9♭5
D-9♭5

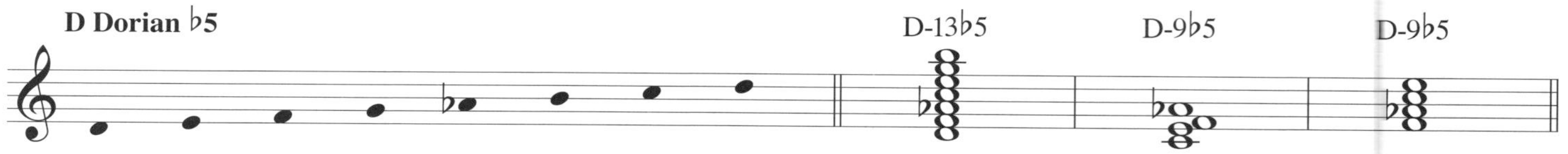

E Phyrgian ♭4

E7♭13(♯9 ♭9)
E7♭13(♯9)
E7♭13(♯9)

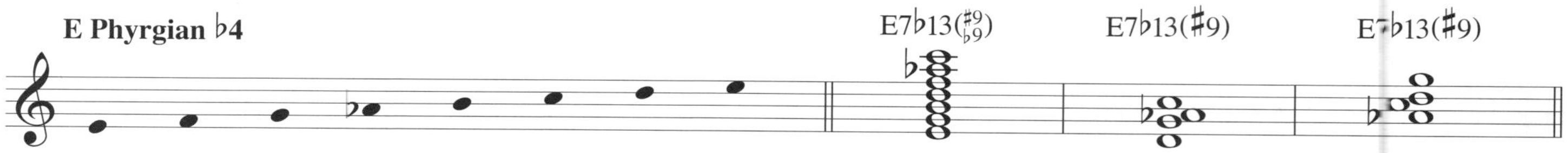

F minor Lydian-Ionian

F-13♯11(Δ7)
F-9♯11(Δ7)
F-9♯11(Δ7)

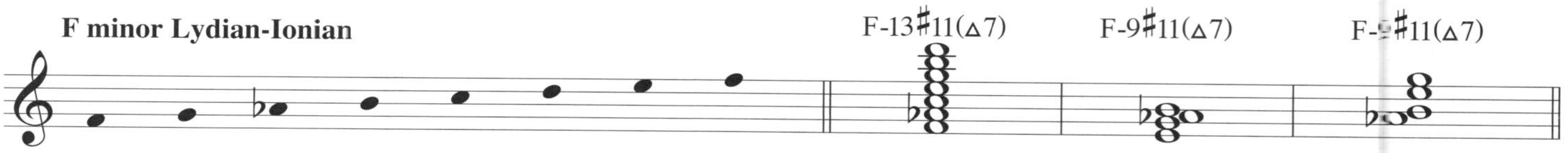

G Mixolydian ♭9

G13(♭9)
G13(♭9)
G13♭9

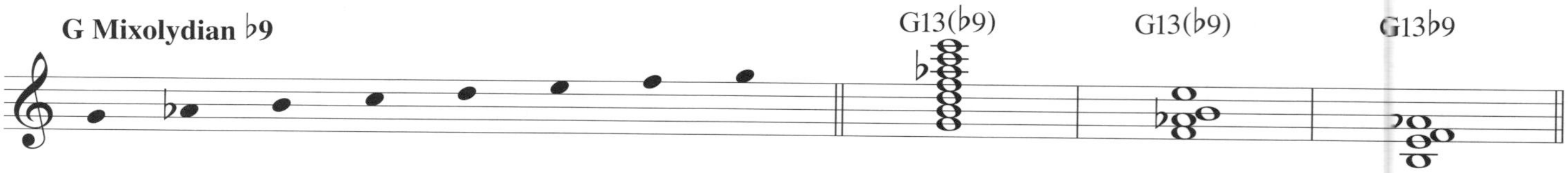

A♭ Lydian "Split Third" ♯5

A♭13♯11(♯9 ♯5)
A♭Δ7♯9(♯5)
A♭7♯9(♯5)

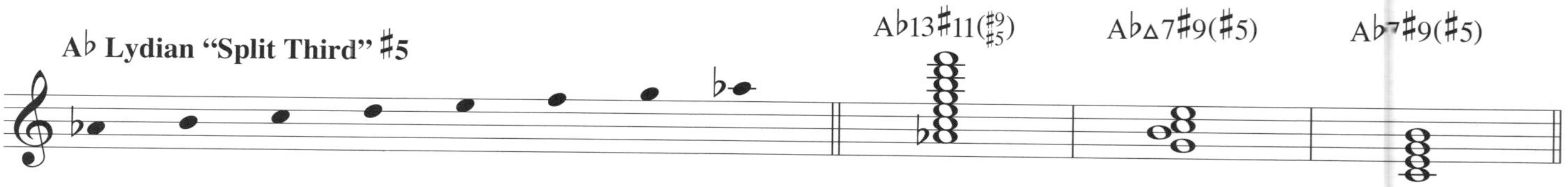

B Locrian ♭7

Bdim11♭13(♭9)
Bdim7♭13(♭9)
Bdim7♭13(♭9)

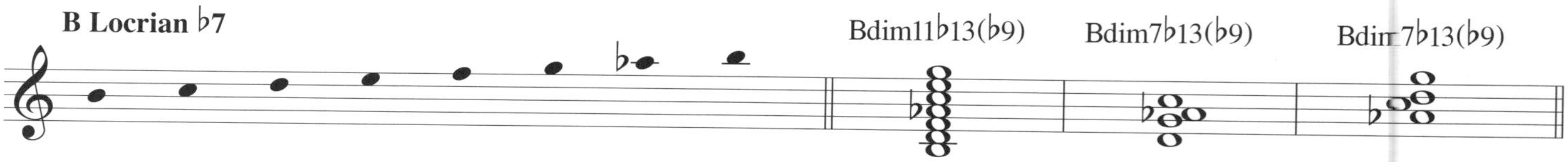

Harmonic Major Etude Over a Bird Blues

Practice this exercise on your instrument. Start slowly, gradually increasing the tempo over time.

PLAYING EXERCISES

Practice each etude with a metronome, gradually increasing the tempo over a period of days and weeks. Work toward ♩ = 120.

Bird Blues Descending Outline – Basic

Bird Blues Descending Outline – Advanced

Bird Blues Harmonic Major Etude

Bird Blues Harmonic Major Stepwise Diatonic Transposition Study

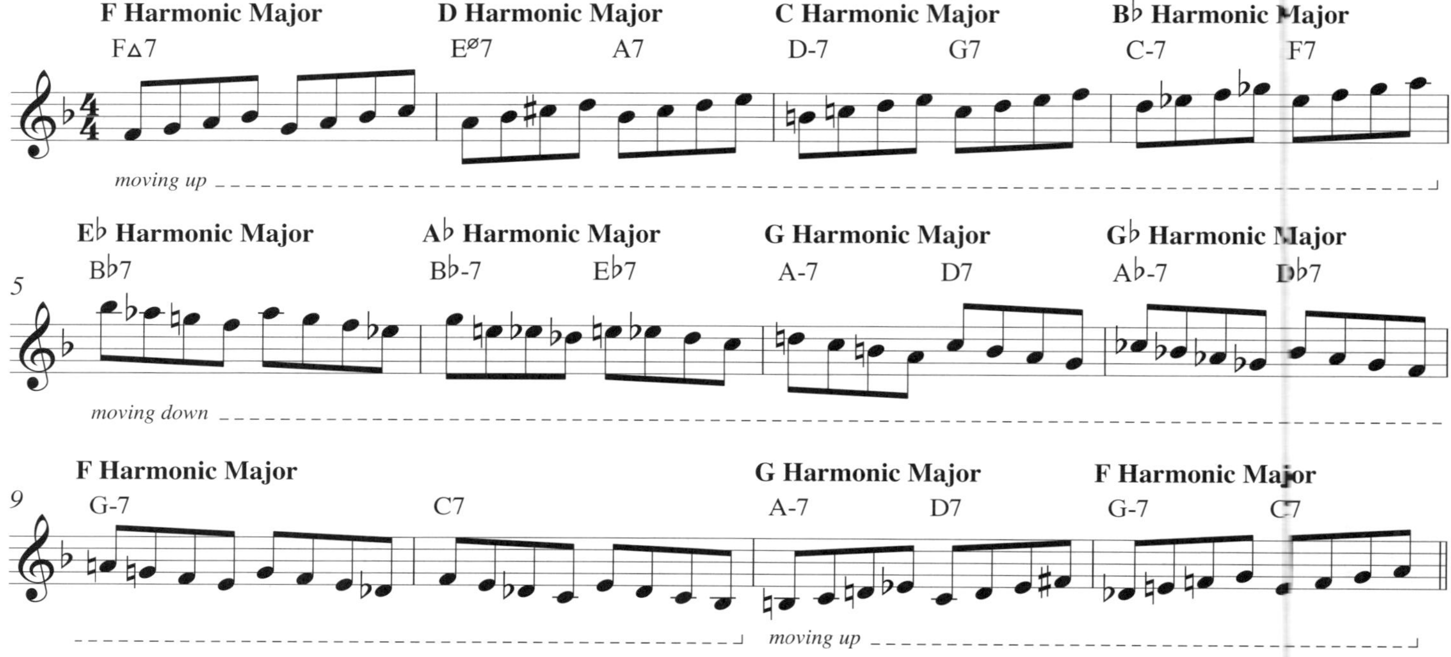

Bird Blues Harmonic Major Treatment (IV)

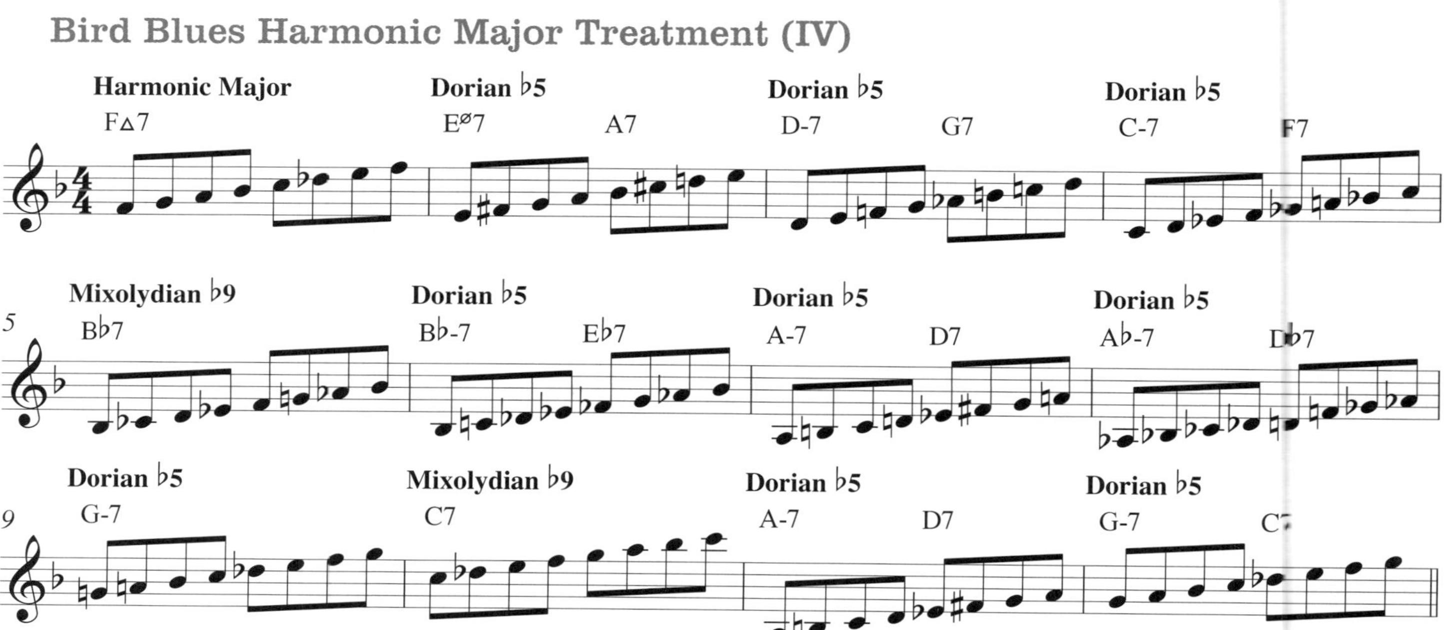

Bird Blues Harmonic Major Treatment (V)

CHAPTER 12

MINOR BLUES

Concepts, Scales, and Modes

- Dorian Mode
- Melodic Minor (& Altered Scale)
- Natural Minor
- Harmonic Minor

This chapter concentrates on various "minor" modes. Herein are exercises that will help you explore sounds found in bebop harmony and commonly used in modern improvisation. The concepts will develop aural correlations with the sound of minor scales with minor, dominant, and altered chords as and will increase your technical facility to work inside and outside of those structures. **Remember:** Do not move on to other exercises until you have mastered each concept. You can do it!

ABOUT MODES

Modes can be used not only on minor chords, but also on those with major, dominant, suspended (sus), and altered qualities. This superimposition of modes over different chord qualities offers additional harmonic options on both symmetrical structures (diminished and/or augmented triads) and asymmetrical structures (everything else). As is the case with other modes, the minor modes are derived by playing the minor scale starting on different scale degrees.

DORIAN SCALE

The Dorian scale is the second mode of the major scale. It can be used to play on the minor chord in a major ii–V pattern (e.g., Cm7, as seen in previous chapters), but also can be used to tonicize a minor I chord.

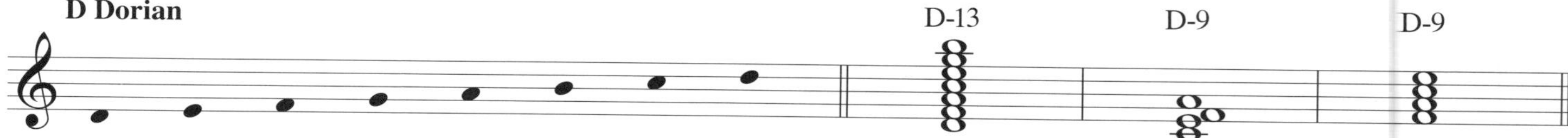

MELODIC MINOR SCALE

The melodic minor scale has two different forms. In its ascending form, the 3rd is lowered, while the 6th and 7th scale degrees are raised. In its descending form, the scale is identical to natural minor. In jazz, the melodic minor scale is the same ascending and descending. It will retain the lowered 3rd, natural 6th and natural 7th in both the ascending and descending forms.

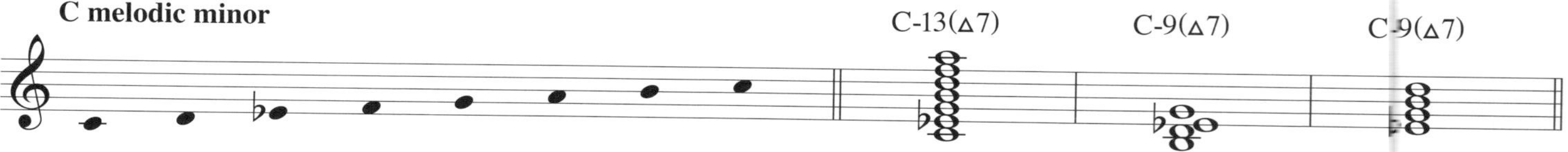

Melodic Minor Scales – Unison

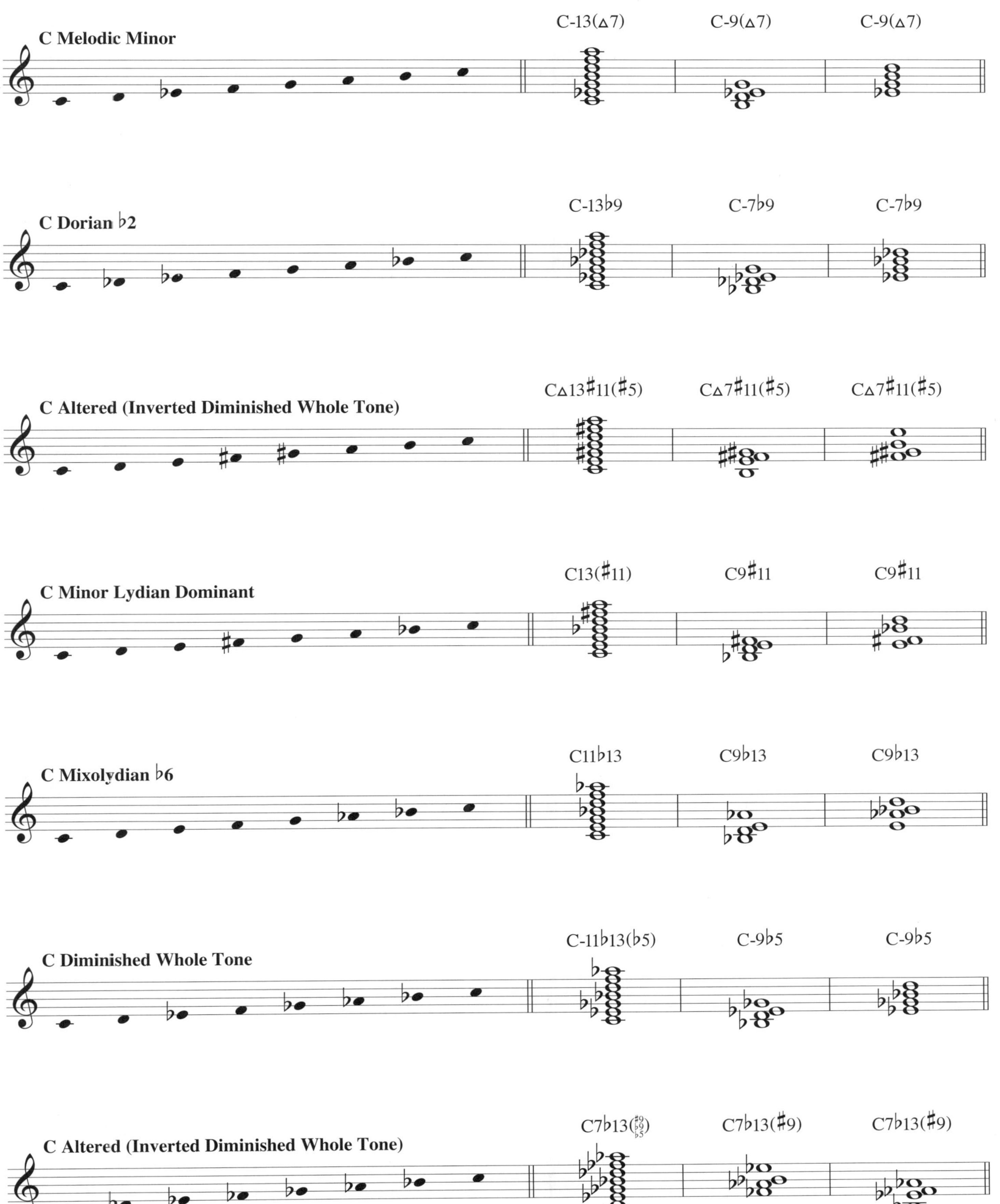

Melodic Minor Scales – Diatonic

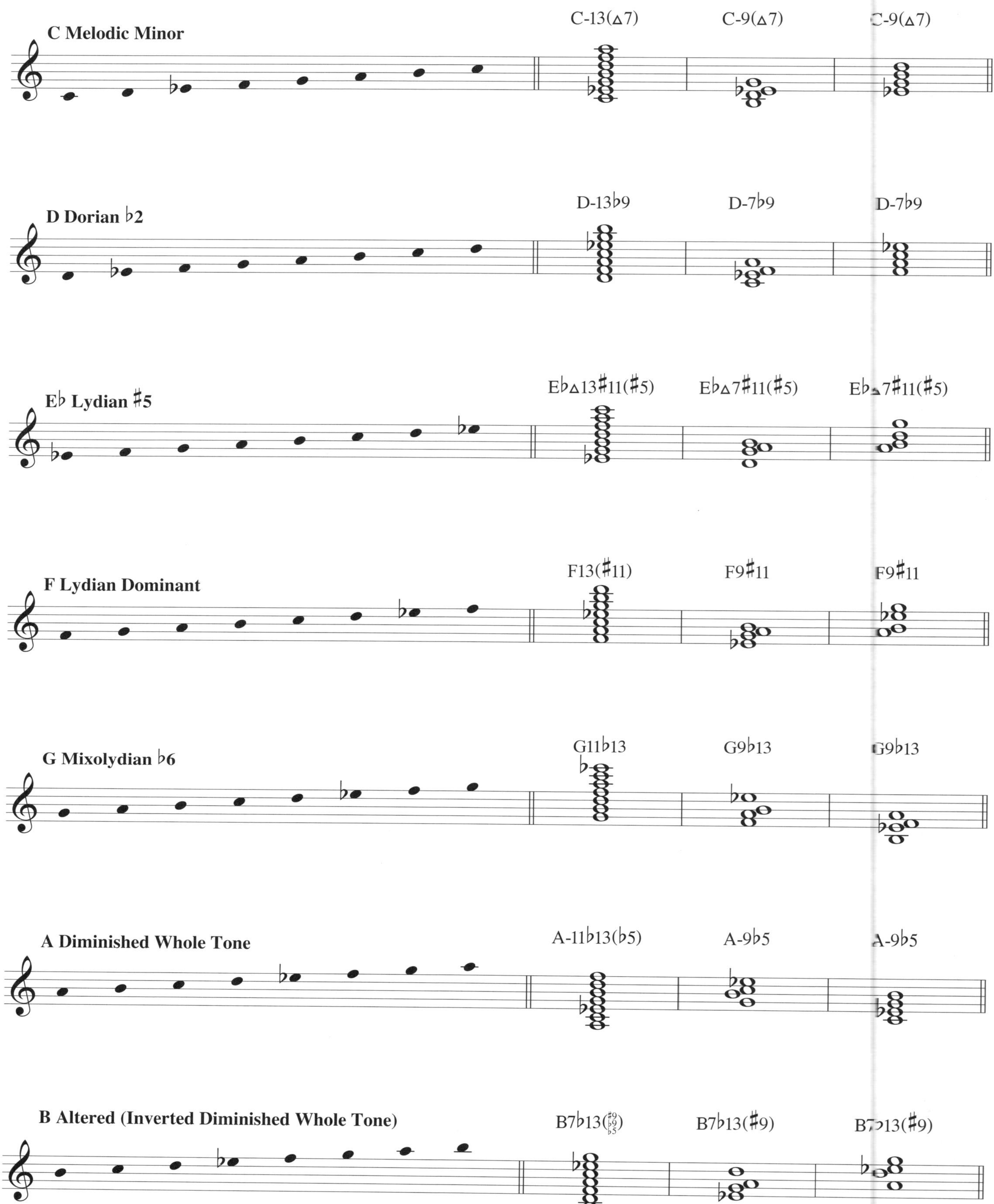

ALTERED SCALE

The altered scale (a.k.a. inverted diminished/whole-tone scale) is the seventh mode of melodic minor. It can be used to play all the alterations of an altered-dominant chord (♯9, ♭9, ♯11, ♯5, ♭5, ♭13); the scale can be superimposed over any kind of altered dominant chord.

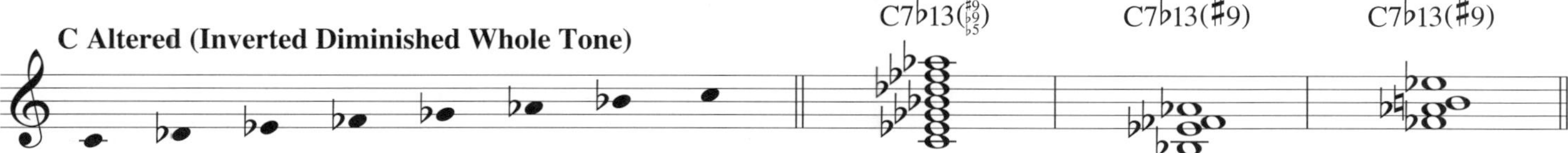

NATURAL MINOR SCALE

Natural minor (Aeolian) is the sixth mode of the major scale. Natural minor can be used to tonicize a minor I chord, not unlike Dorian. Although it has been a long-standing practice in jazz to use Dorian to tonicize the minor I, from a functional perspective, natural minor is a more accurate choice.

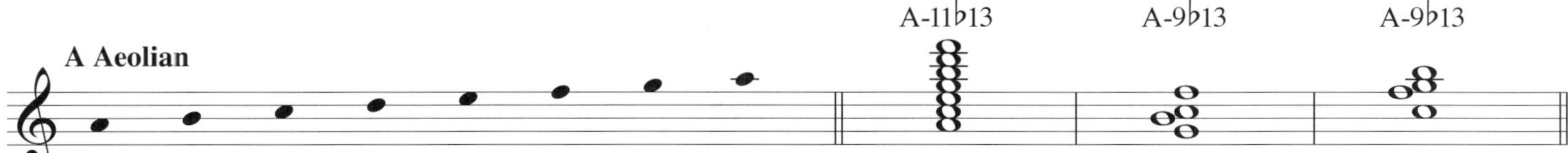

HARMONIC MINOR SCALE

The harmonic minor scale is another option to tonicize a minor I chord. The scale is constructed using a lowered 3rd, lowered 6th, and raised 7th.

PLAYING EXERCISES

Practice each etude with a metronome, gradually increasing the tempo over a period of days and weeks. Work toward ♩ = 120.

Dorian Blues Scale Study – Ascending

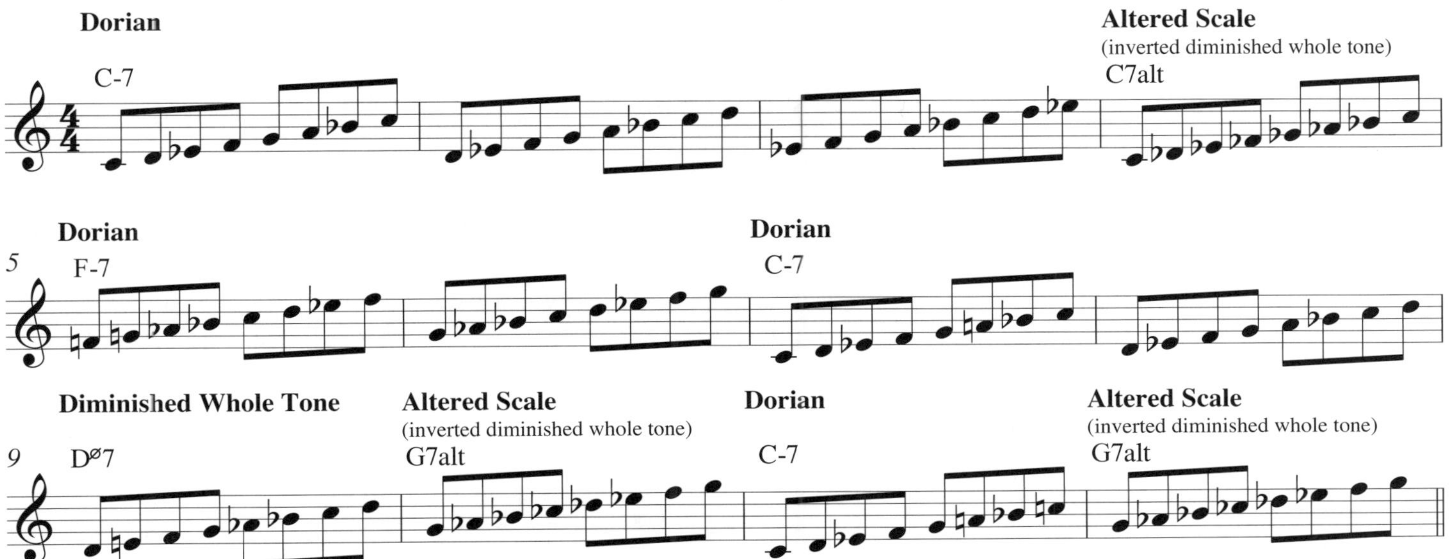

Melodic Minor Blues Scale Study – Ascending
Melodic Minor
C-(△7)
Dorian ♭2
G-7♭9
C7♭13
5
Melodic Minor
F-(△7)
Melodic Minor
C-(△7)
9
Dorian ♭2
D-7♭9
Mixolydian ♭13
G7♭13
Melodic Minor
C-(△7)
Mixolydian ♭13
G7♭13
Natural Minor Blues Scale Study – Ascending
Natural Minor
C-7♭13
Locrian
Gø7
Natural Minor
F-7♭13
Natural Minor
C-7♭13
9
Locrian
Dø7
Phrygian
G7sus(♭9)
Natural Minor
C-7♭13
Phrygian
G7sus(♭9)
Minor Blues Diminished Study – Coltrane Pattern
C-6
Retrograde Pattern
(diminished scale)
C-6
Inverted Ascending Pattern
(diminished scale)
C7alt
Retrograde Pattern
(inverted diminished scale)
C7alt
Inverted Ascending Pattern
(inverted diminished scale)
1. F-6 Dø7
2. G7alt
1. Retrograde Pattern
(diminished scale)
2. Retrograde Pattern
(inverted diminished scale)
1. F-6 Dø7
2. G7alt
1. Inverted Ascending Pattern
(diminished scale)
2. Inverted Ascending Pattern
(inverted diminished scale)

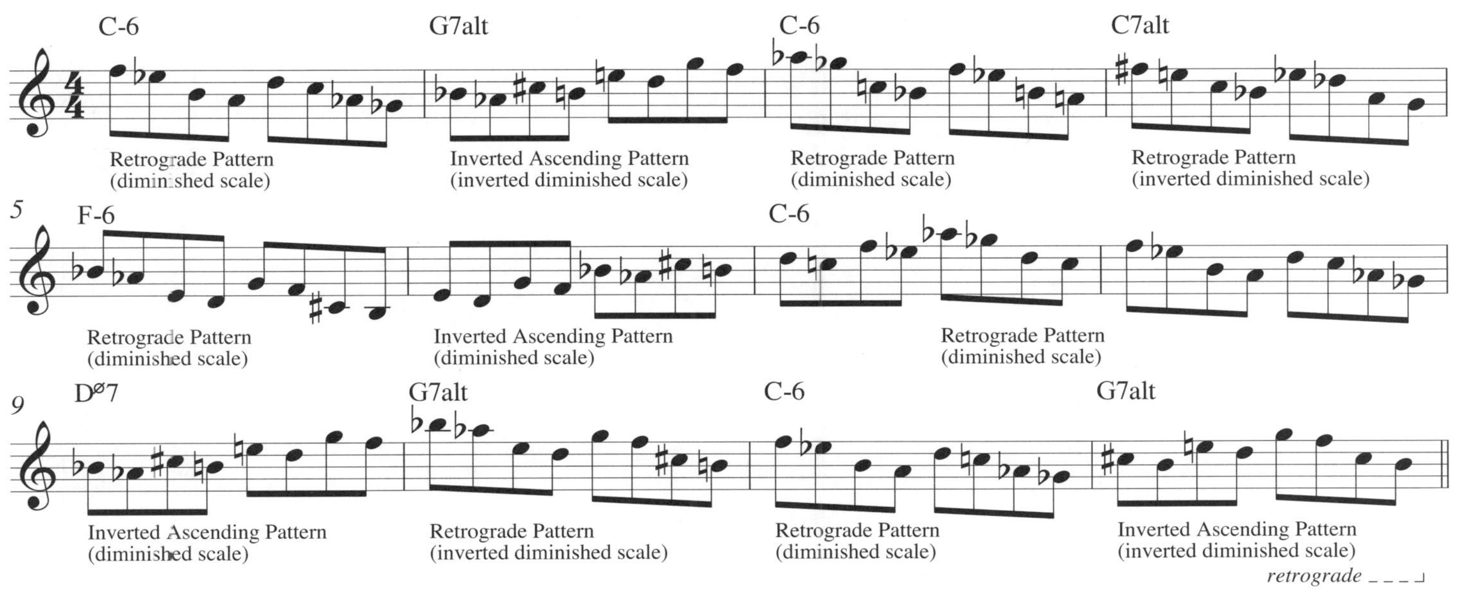

Harmonic Minor Blues Continuous Diatonic 7th Study

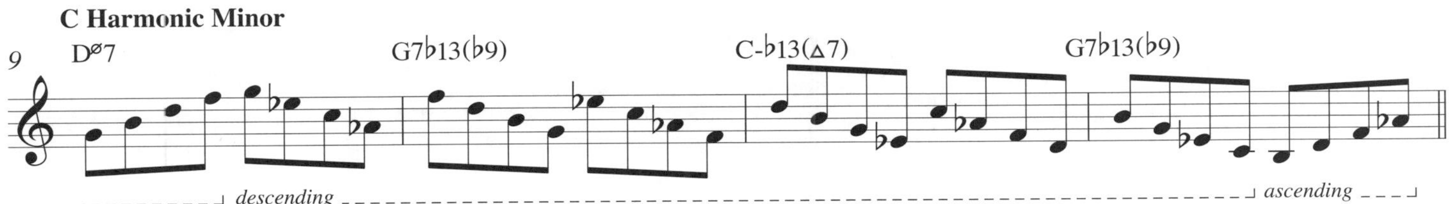

Minor Blues Approximate Enclosure Study

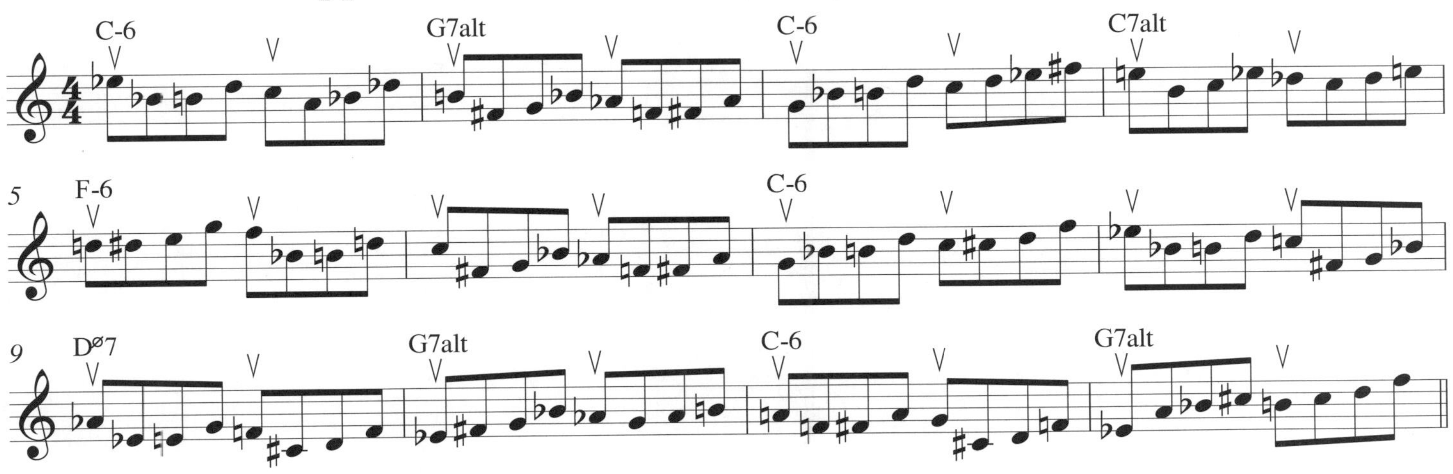

Minor Blues Augmented Pattern Study

CHAPTER 13

TRIAD PAIRS

Concepts, Scales, and Modes

- Triad Pairs

In this chapter, we'll concentrate on *triad pairs*. Triad pairs are used by modern improvisers to broaden the scope of material to play, even while limiting note choices to two triads. Using triad pairs can help you approach chord changes from a fresh perspective and provide a systematic means to improve intervallic improvisation. The concepts here will allow you to explore sounds created by limiting improvisation to specific triad pairs. While incorporating larger intervals into your solos, you'll increase both your technical facility and your understanding of chord changes. **Remember:** Do not move on to other exercises until you have mastered each concept. You can do it!

ABOUT TRIAD PAIRS

A triad pair is made up of any two triads that have no notes in common. Triad pairs are a great way of incorporating larger intervals into solos specifically defining two separate constructs (a.k.a. working bitonally). Triad pairs can serve as a basis to form melodic and intervallic patterns using hexatonic (six-note) structures.

Creating Triad Pairs

Triad pairs can be created in a number of ways. In major modes, they are constructed by building triads from the fourth and fifth degrees of a scale. The notes in the triad are diatonic to the scale used to make the pair. For example, a triad pair from a C major scale is built from F (fourth scale degree) and G (fifth scale degree) and uses notes diatonic to a C major scale – in this case, F major and G major triads.

The following lists various scales and the triad pairs that work well with them. The scales and triad pairs are shown in the examples that follow.

- Major, Minor, Harmonic Minor, Melodic Minor (4th, 5th)
- Harmonic Major (5th, ♭6th)
- Whole Tone (root, 2nd)
- Diminished (M7, 4th)
- Inverted Diminished (root, tritone)
- Augmented (M7, root)
- Inverted Augmented (root, ♭2)

Scale Families and Triad Pairs

Building a triad pair when faced with a particular chord

"Scale family" is the scale from which the mode is based. For example F Dorian's scale family is E♭ major. E augmented/Phrygian's scale family is G harmonic minor. E♭ Lydian/Mixolydian's scale family is B♭ melodic minor. Once the mode is associated with the chord for improvisation, determine the scale family. That scale family will define the triad pair.

Eight Ways to Play a Pattern: Triad Pairs

In Chapter 3, you had the chance to learn eight different ways to play a pattern. When learning triad pairs, you have the same opportunity. In practice, there are eight different ways to play triad pairs.

- **ascending:** ascending motif
- **retrograde:** motif played with notes descending
- **inverted ascending:** descending motif played ascending
- **inverted retrograde:** ascending motif played descending
- **alternating ascending:** ascending motif followed by a descending motif (ascending version)
- **alternating retrograde:** descending motif followed by ascending motif (descending version)
- **inverted alternating ascending:** inverted motif followed by inverted retrograde motif (ascending version)
- **inverted alternating retrograde:** inverted motif followed by inverted retrograde motif (descending version)

Eight Ways to Play a Pattern: Three-Note Pairs

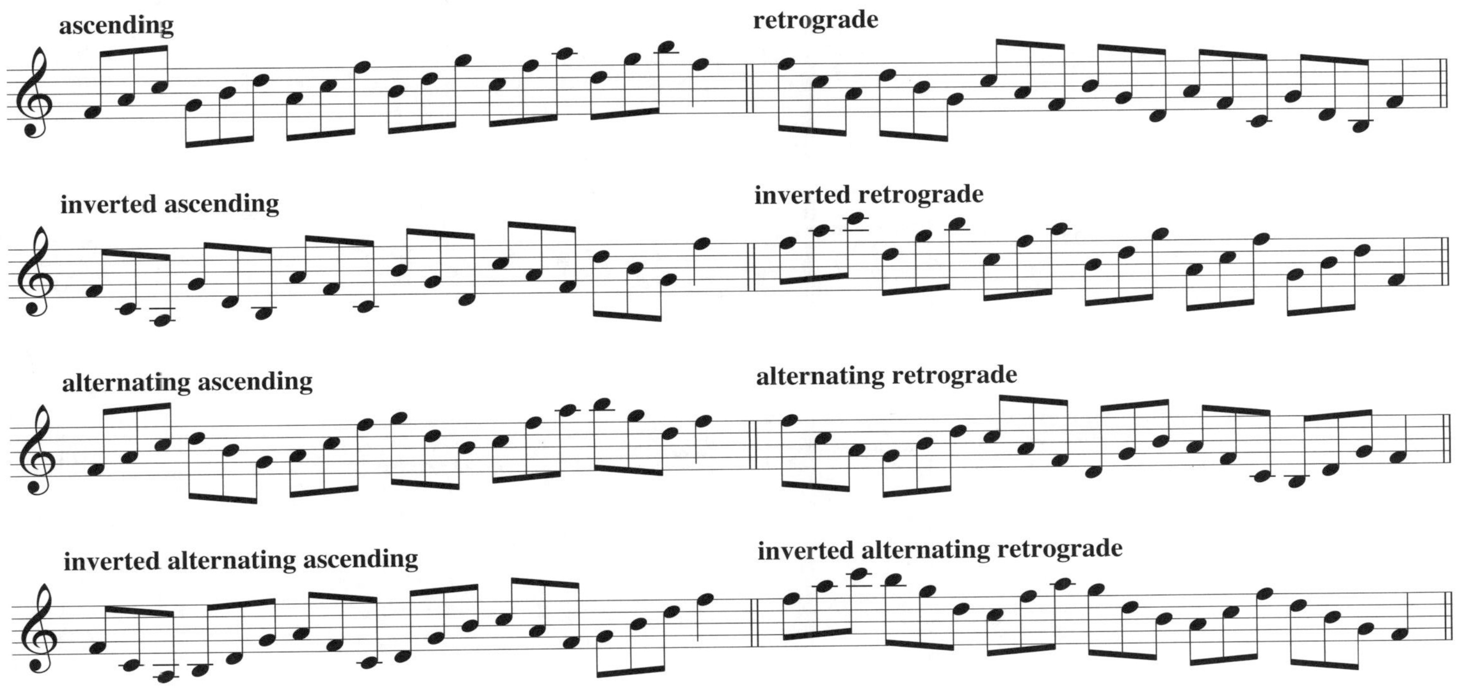

Eight Ways to Play a Pattern: Four-Note Pairs

PLAYING EXERCISES

Triad pairs can sometimes sound too mechanical. The goal of these exercises is to develop control and flexibility with triad pairs so you can employ them anywhere. Practice each etude with a metronome, gradually increasing the tempo over a period of days and weeks. Work toward ♩ = 120.

Bird Blues Harmonic Major Family Triad Pair
Exercise 1 – Root Relationship

Bird Blues Harmonic Major Family Triad Pair
Exercise 2 – Unison Relationship

Bird Blues Harmonic Major Family Triad Pair Exercise 3 – Stepwise Relationship

Bird Blues Triad Pair Etude #1

Blues Diminished Scale Family Triad Pair Study 1 – Root Relationship

Blues Diminished Scale Family Triad Pair Study 2 – Unison Relationship

Blues Diminished Scale Family Triad Pair Study 3 – Stepwise Relationship

Blues Major Scale Family Guide Tone Study 1 – Root Relationship

Blues Major Scale Family Guide Tone Study 2 – Unison Relationship

Blues Major Scale Family Guide Tone Study 3 – Stepwise Relationship

Blues Major Scale Family Triad Pair Study 1 – Root Relationship

Pattern for Exercise

Blues Major Scale Family Triad Pair Study 2 – Unison Relationship

Blues Major Scale Family Triad Pair Study 3 – Stepwise Relationship

Minor Blues Harmonic Minor Scale Family Triad Pair Study 1 – Root Relationship

Minor Blues Harmonic Minor Scale Family Triad Pair Study 2 – Unison Relationship

Minor Blues Harmonic Minor Scale Family Triad Pair Study 3 – Stepwise Relationship

Minor Blues Melodic Minor Scale Family Triad Pair Study 1 – Root Relationship

Minor Blues Melodic Minor Scale Family Triad Pair Study 2 – Unison Relationship

Minor Blues Melodic Minor Scale Family Triad Pair Study 3 – Stepwise Relationship

CHAPTER 14
RHYTHM CHANGES

Concepts, Scales, and Modes

- About Rhythm Changes
- Canvas Approach to Rhythm Changes
- Rhythm Changes – Using Church Modes

In this chapter you will concentrate on applying chord-scale theory to rhythm changes chord progressions. The exercises here will help you learn to utilize church modes (see page 28) within Rhythm Changes and increase technical facility therein. **Remember:** Do not move on to other exercises until you have mastered each concept. You can do it!

ABOUT RHYTHM CHANGES

As we noted in Chapter 2 (page 19), Rhythm Changes originates from George Gershwin's song "I Got Rhythm." Over time, the song – or, more appropriately, its chord progression – has become one of the most common vehicles for improvisation. Rhythm Changes serves as foundation for numerous jazz compositions, such as Duke Ellington's "Cotton Tail," Dizzy Gillespie's "Salt Peanuts," and Thelonious Monk's "Rhythm-a-Ning," among countless others. The endurance of the song form can be credited, in large part, to its extensive use as the basis for composition and improvisation by early bebop musicians. Many of these new contrafacts (melodies written over existing chord changes) have become staples of jazz repertoire. The following are a few examples:

- "Anthropology" (Charlie Parker/Dizzy Gillespie)
- "Cotton Tail" (Duke Ellington)
- "Lester Leaps In" (Lester Young)
- "Meet the Flintstones" (Hoyt Curtin)
- "Moose the Mooche" (Charlie Parker)
- "Oleo" (Sonny Rollins)
- "Rhythm-a-Ning" (Thelonious Monk)
- "Steeplechase" (Charlie Parker)

Rhythm Changes: Structure

The Rhythm Changes structure is comprised of 32 measures of music. These measures are separated into four sections. The song form is AABA – meaning that in three of the eight-measure sections, those labeled as "A," the melody and chord changes are exactly the same. Only one section, labeled "B," contains differing harmonic and melodic material.

Rhythm Changes: Classic/Simple Version

The simplest form of Rhythm Changes, one that closely follows the original chords of "I Got Rhythm," is rarely played. The chord changes are as follows:

Rhythm Changes: Common Variation

(Bop Era: Common Practice)

A common variation on Rhythm Changes closely follows the original chords of Gershwin's song "I Got Rhythm," but incorporates more of the harmonic structures common to jazz and jazz improvisation. Rhythm Changes exercises in this text are based on the Bop Era: Common Practice structure.

Rhythm Changes: Substitutions

Further variations to Rhythm Changes include the use of additional chords through practices such as tritone substitution. Here is an example of tritone substitution applied to the "B" section:

Rhythm Changes "B" Section: Common

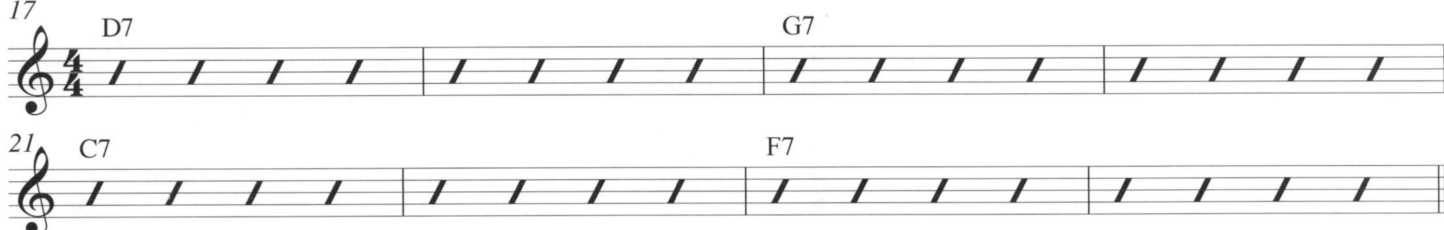

Rhythm Changes "B" Section: Tritone Substitution #1

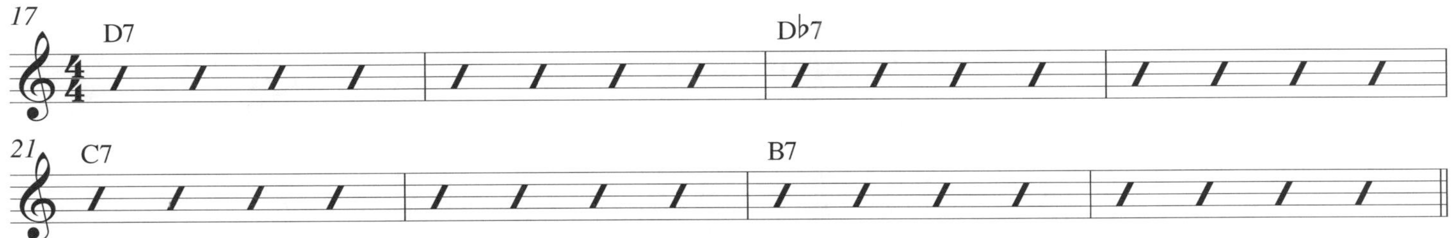

Rhythm Changes "B" Section: Tritone Substitution #2

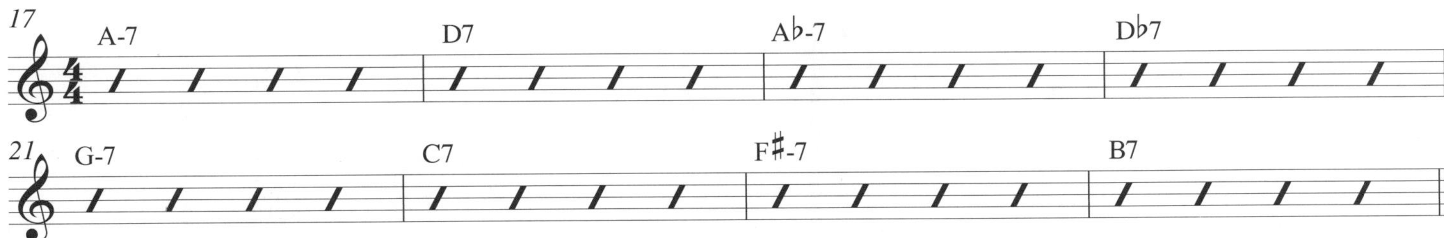

PLAYING RHYTHM CHANGES USING A CANVAS APPROACH WITH CHURCH MODES

Here, we employ scales that are diatonic to each chord, those derived through variations on the major scale (Ionian, Dorian, Mixolydian, etc.) with no additional changes or alterations.

Rhythm Changes: Church Modes "A" section

Rhythm Changes: Church Modes "B" section

17
D7
G7
bebop dominant
21
C7
F7

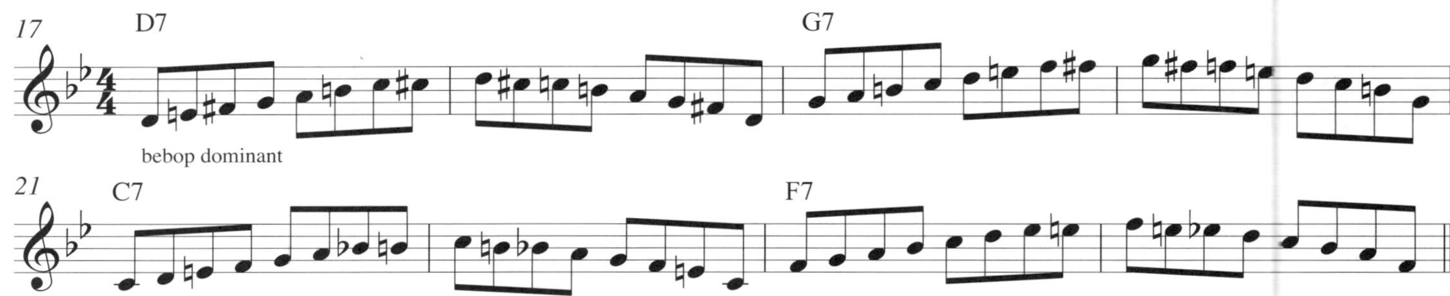

PLAYING EXERCISES

Practice each etude with a metronome, gradually increasing the tempo over a period of days and weeks. Work toward ♩ = 150.

Rhythm Changes Church Mode Study

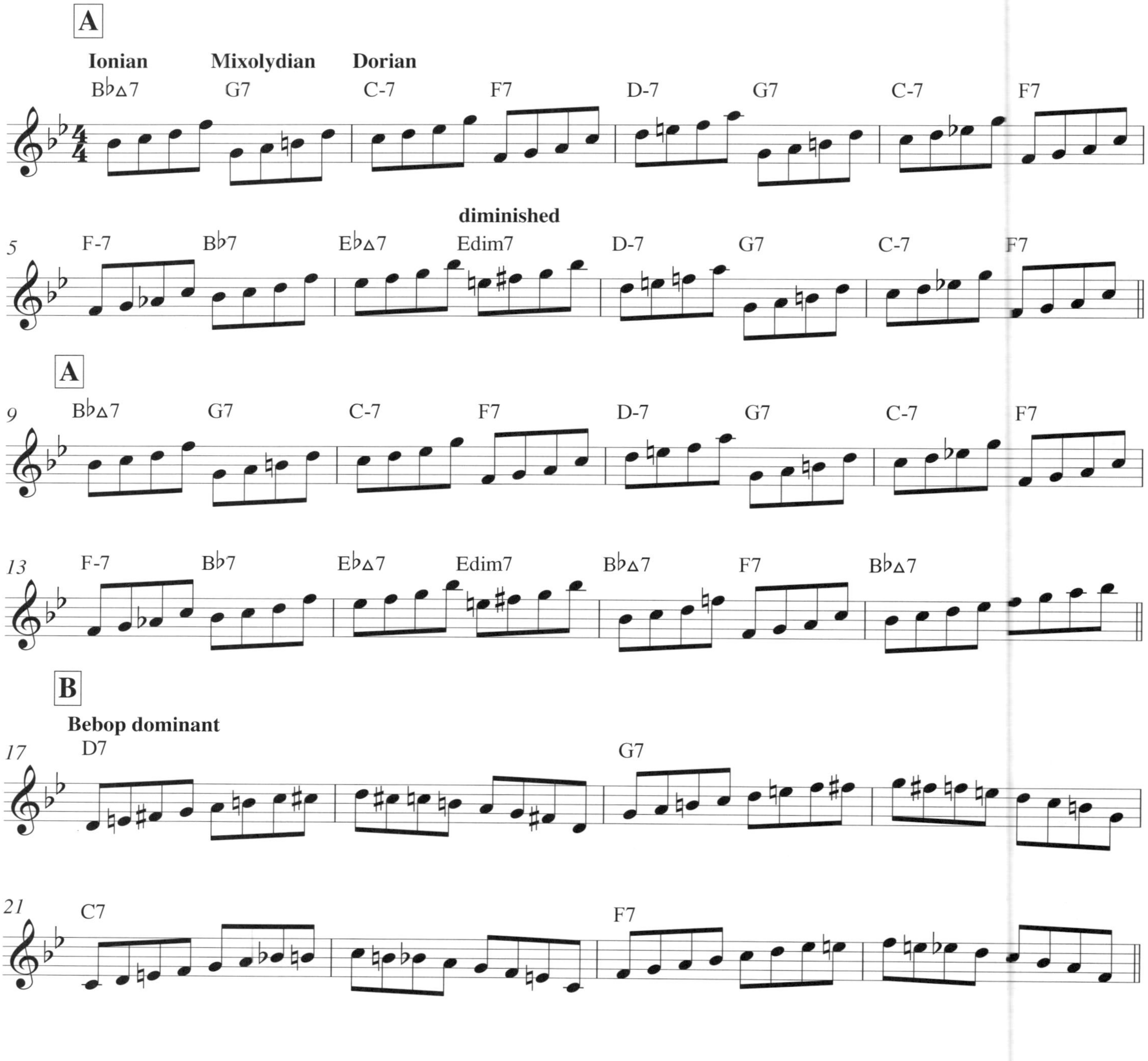

A
Ionian
Mixolydian
Dorian
B♭△7
G7
C-7
F7
D-7
G7
C-7
F7
diminished
5
F-7
B♭7
E♭△7
Edim7
D-7
G7
C-7
F7
A
9
B♭△7
G7
C-7
F7
D-7
G7
C-7
F7
13
F-7
B♭7
E♭△7
Edim7
B♭△7
F7
B♭△7
B
Bebop dominant
17
D7
G7
21
C7
F7

A
25 B♭△7 G7 C-7 F7 D-7 G7 C-7 F7
29 F-7 B♭7 E♭△7 Edim7 B♭△7 F7 B♭△7

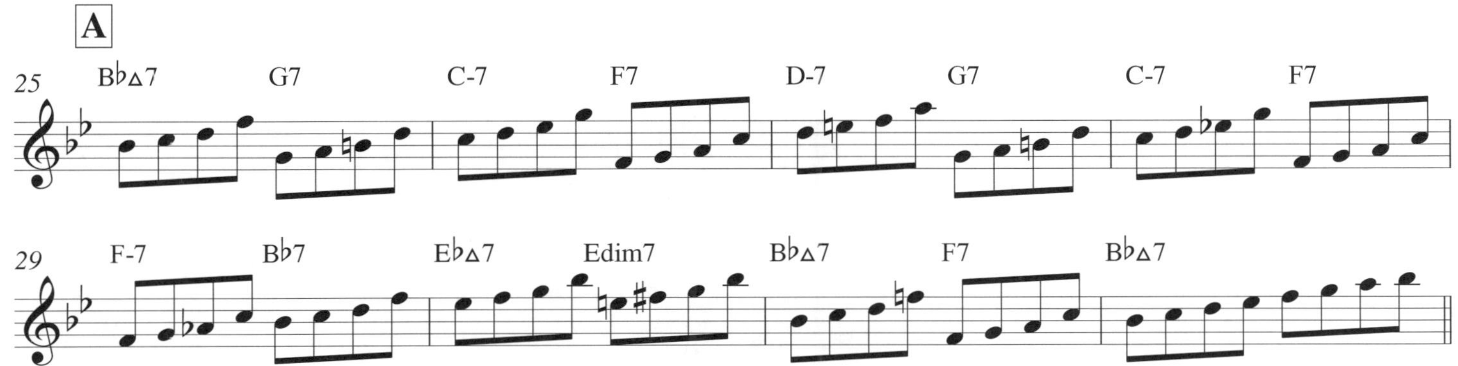

Rhythm Changes Church Mode Study – Retrograde

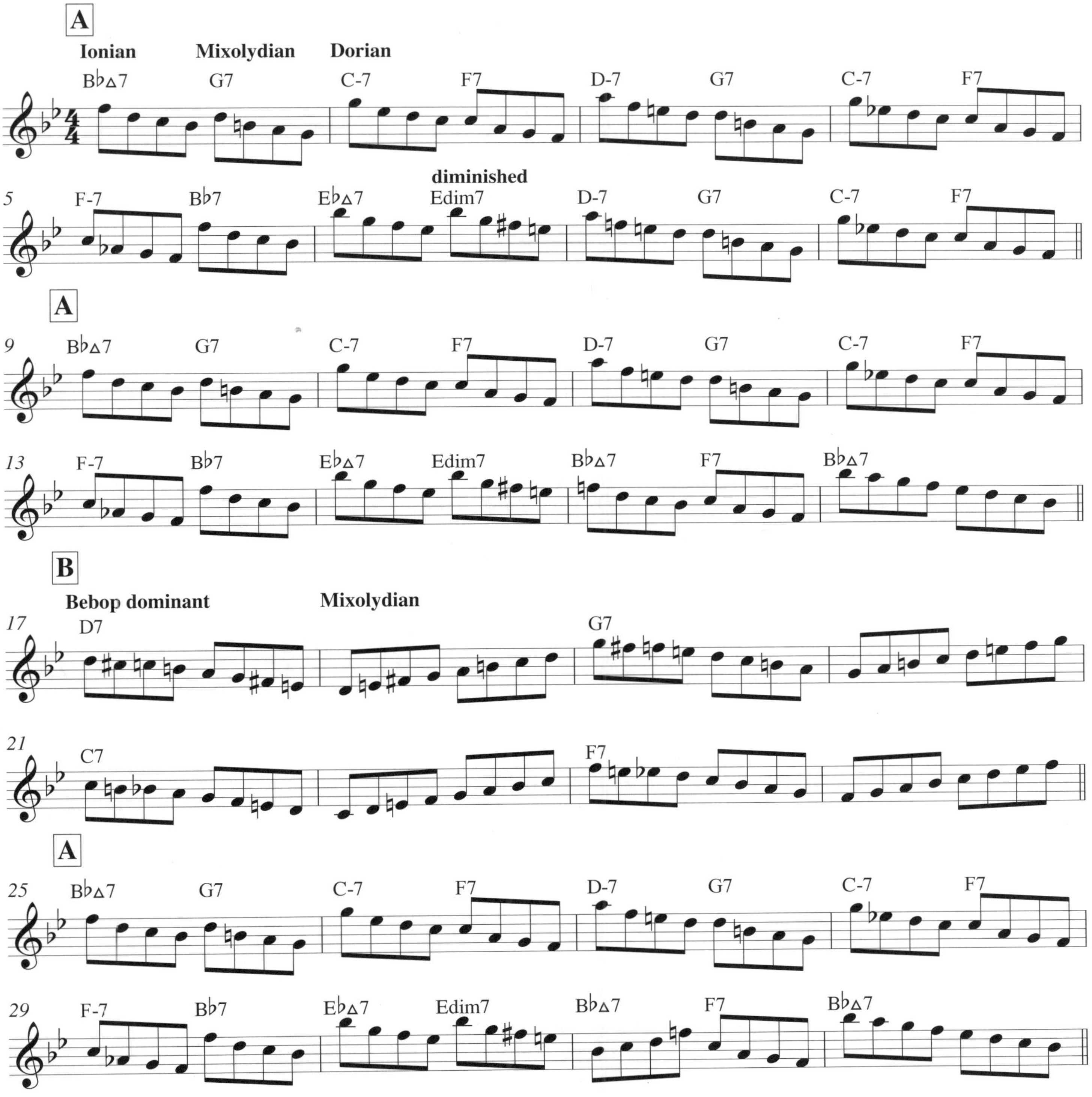
A
Ionian
Mixolydian
Dorian
B♭△7 G7 C-7 F7 D-7 G7 C-7 F7
diminished
5 F-7 B♭7 E♭△7 Edim7 D-7 G7 C-7 F7
A
9 B♭△7 G7 C-7 F7 D-7 G7 C-7 F7
13 F-7 B♭7 E♭△7 Edim7 B♭△7 F7 B♭△7
B
Bebop dominant
Mixolydian
17 D7 G7
21 C7 F7
A
25 B♭△7 G7 C-7 F7 D-7 G7 C-7 F7
29 F-7 B♭7 E♭△7 Edim7 B♭△7 F7 B♭△7

Rhythm Changes Church Mode Study – Alternating (A)

Rhythm Changes Church Mode Study – Alternating (B)

Rhythm Changes Church Mode Continuous Scales Study

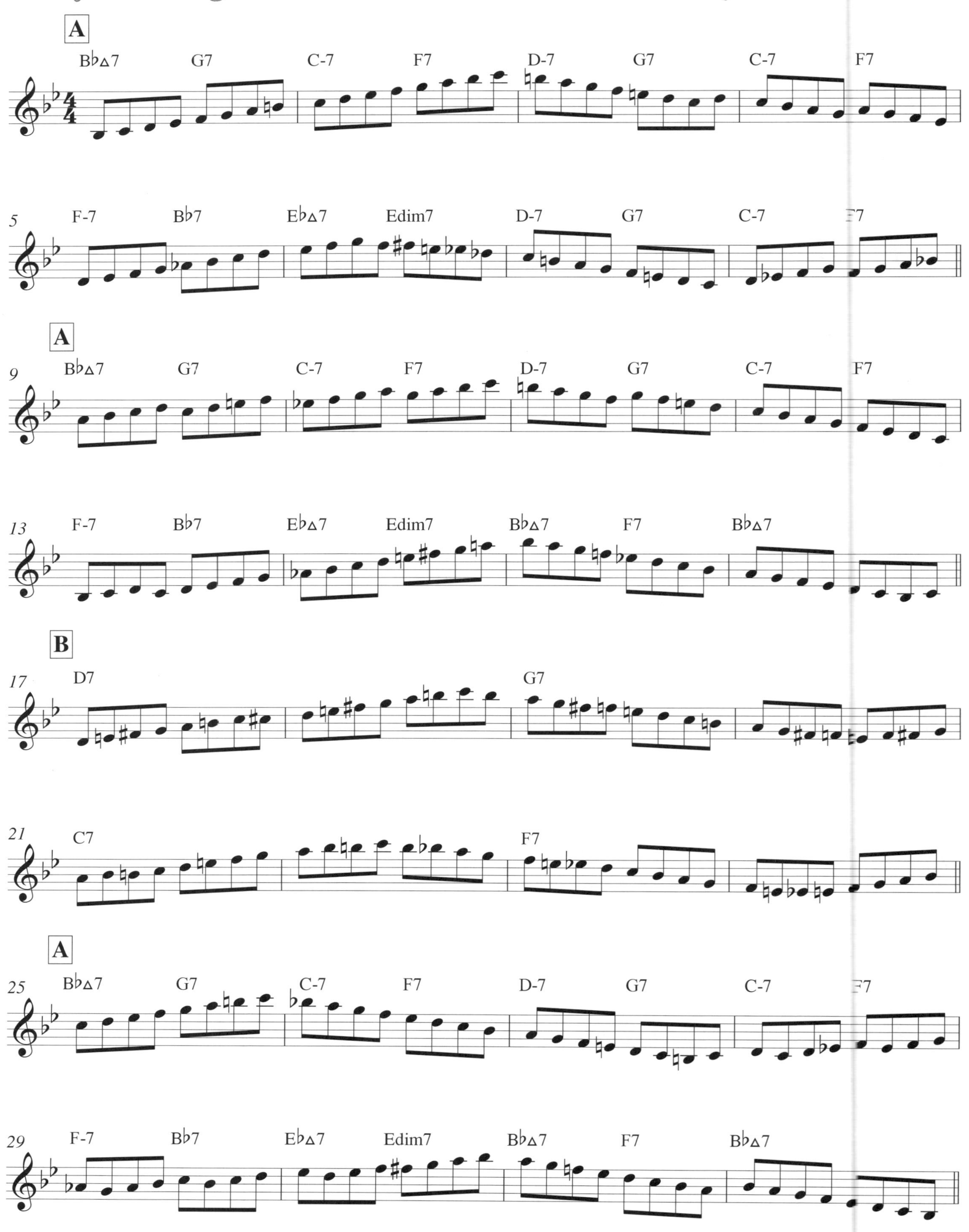

CHAPTER 15
RHYTHM CHANGES – BEBOP SCALES

Concepts, Scales & Modes

- Bebop Scales Approach to Rhythm Changes

In this chapter, you will concentrate on applying chord-scale theory to Rhythm Changes chord progressions. The exercises will help you utilize bebop scales within Rhythm Changes and increase technical facility therein. **Remember:** Do not move on to other exercises until you have mastered each concept. You can do it!

ABOUT BEBOP SCALES: REVIEW

In this text, the term *bebop scales* refers to those that are diatonic to a mode and possess an added chromatic passing tone. The chromatic passing tone may appear anywhere in the scale that a half step can be put between whole steps; it is not restricted to a singular location in the scale (e.g., between the seventh scale degree and the root). The major scale, for example, contains seven modes from which bebop scales can be derived. Within each major mode, there are five locations in which a chromatic passing tone can be inserted; the chromatic passing tone is inserted in only one of the five locations. This same pattern exists in modes of melodic minor modes, harmonic minor, and harmonic major. In total, there are 140 different bebop scales available to the improvisers utilizing this concept.

Here are the bebop scales that can be derived from a C major scale:

- **C Ionian bebop:** C-D-E-F-G-A-(A♯/B♭)-B
- **D Dorian bebop:** D-E-F-G-A-(A♯)-B-C
- **E Phrygian bebop:** E-F-G-A-(A♯/B♭)-B-C-D
- **F Lydian bebop:** F-G-A-(A♯/B♭)-B-C-D-E
- **G Mixolydian bebop:** G-A-(A♯/B♭)-B-C-D-E-F
- **A Aeolian bebop:** A-(A♯/B♭)-B-C-D-E-F-G
- **B Locrian bebop:** B-C-D-E-F-(F♯/G♭)-G-A

Benefits of Bebop Scales

Bebop scales provide the means to add chromaticism to improvisations in a linear fashion. Additionally, a single chromatic passing tone – depending both on its placement and the use of swung eighths – can lend a variety of weak-beat/strong-beat emphasis. Bebop scales are typically played descending; however, it is important to learn them both ascending and descending to improve technical fluency.

BEBOP SCALES: APPLICATIONS FOR RHYTHM CHANGES

Chromaticism at Fast Tempos

Songs based upon Rhythm Changes are sometimes performed at a brisk tempo (200-350 bpm). This makes bebop scales an excellent means to facilitate fluency at technically demanding tempos. For example:

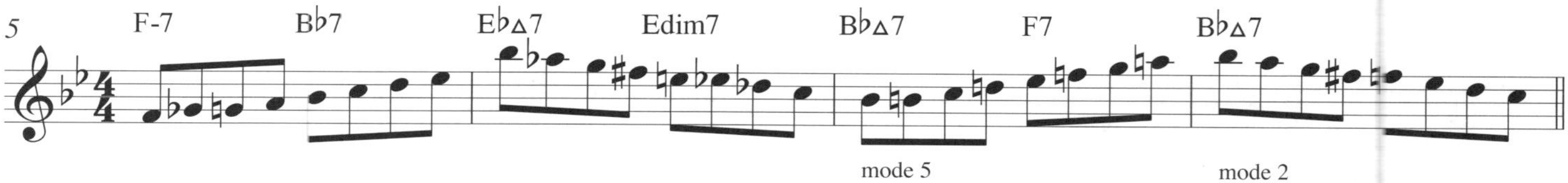

Bebop Scales Over the "B" Section of Rhythm Changes

Bebop scales are part of the accepted canon of bebop vocabulary. Mastery of these scales helps communicate understanding of bebop tradition. They are particularly effective on the "B" section because of the Circle of 4ths motion with dominant chords.

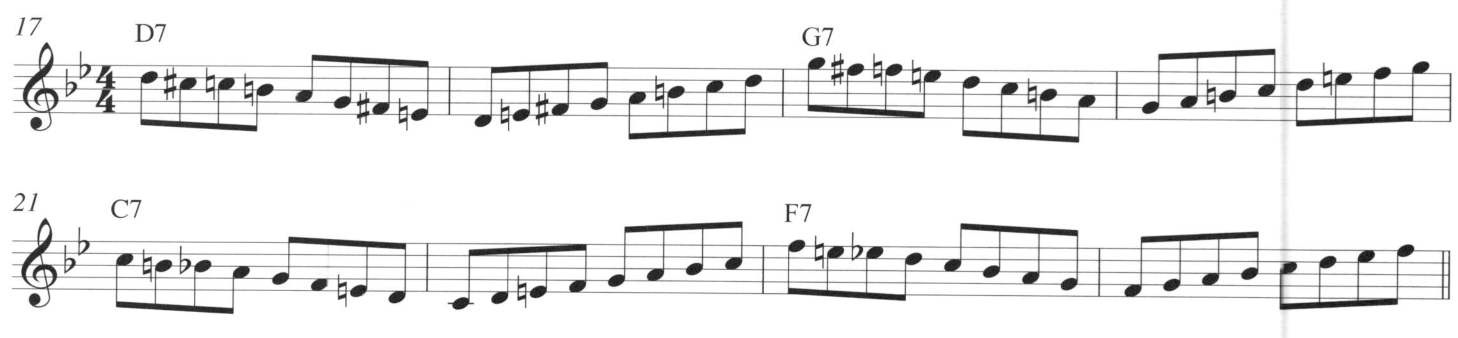

Bebop Scales Over the "A" Section of Rhythm Changes

Bebop scales are also highly useful on cadences (V–I or II–V–I), half cadences (II–V), and turnarounds (III–VI–II–V–I). (See pre-dominant function and dominant function.) Each of these progressions exists in the "A" section of rhythm changes.

PLAYING EXERCISES

Practice each etude with a metronome, gradually increasing the tempo over a period of days and weeks. Work toward ♩ = 150.

Rhythm Changes Bebop Scale Study 1

Rhythm Changes Bebop Scale Study 2

CHAPTER 16

RHYTHM CHANGES – WHOLE-TONE & DIMINISHED SCALES

Concepts, Scales, and Modes

- Whole-Tone Scale Approach to Rhythm Changes
- Diminished Scale Approach to Rhythm Changes

In this chapter, you will concentrate on applying chord-scale theory to Rhythm Changes chord progressions. The exercises will help you utilize whole-tone scales and diminished scales within Rhythm Changes and increase technical facility therein. **Remember:** Do not move on to other exercises until you have mastered each concept. You can do it!

REVIEW: ABOUT WHOLE-TONE SCALES

Whole-tone scales are hexatonic (six-note) scales in which each note is separated from its neighbors by one whole step. Enharmonic spelling of notes within whole-tone scales is common practice. There are two unique whole-tone scales; each scale has six modes. (See page 59.)

Modes of C-D, E-F♯-G♯-A♯ whole-tone scale	**Modes of D♭-E♭-F-G-A-B whole-tone scale**
Db whole tone: D♭-E♭-F-G-A-B	C whole tone: C-D-E-F♯-G♯-A♯
Eb whole tone: E♭-F-G-A-B-D♭	D whole tone: D-E-F♯-G♯-A♯-C
F whole tone: F-G-A-B-C♯(D♭)-D♯(E♭)	E whole tone: E-F♯-G♯-A♯-C-D
G whole tone: G-A-B-C♯(D♭)-D♯(E♭)-F	F♯ whole tone: F♯-G♯-A♯-C-D-E
A whole tone: A-B-C♯(D♭)-D♯(E♭)-F-G	G♯ whole tone: G♯-A♯-B♯(C)-D-E-F♯
	A♯ whole tone: A♯-B♯(C)-D-E-F♯-G♯
	B whole tone: B-C♯(D♭)-D♯(E♭)-F-G-A

Benefits of Whole-Tone Scales

Whole-tone scales have limited transposition (there are only two transpositions). However, they are one of the most commonly used scales on altered dominant chords, alongside the altered scale and inverted diminished scale.

WHOLE-TONE SCALES

Applications for Rhythm Changes

In the context of Rhythm Changes, whole-tone scales are best applied to dominant-seventh (V7) chords. They are especially effective on the "B" section, in which scales can have a unison relationship with the chord presented (e.g., F7 = F whole-tone). It is important to note that, in this context, application of the whole-tone scale infers functions of change of the harmony or the use of alterations on the chord (e.g., D7 with D whole-tone applied = D7♯5, D7♯11(♯5), or D7♯11).

Rhythm Changes Example 1: Whole-Tone Over the "B" Section

Within the context of Rhythm Changes, whole-tone scales are applicable on half cadences (II–V), cadences (II–V–I), and turnarounds (III–VI–II–V–I).

Rhythm Changes Example 2: Whole-Tone Over the "A" Section

In the case of the II–V–I and III–VI–II–V–I, avoid playing the whole-tone scale on the I chord. However, apply whole-tone scales with dominant function on II–V, II–V–I and III–VI–II–V–I (Dm7–G7–Cm7–F7–B♭: Use F whole-tone scale and resolve on the B♭ major chord.)

REVIEW: ABOUT DIMINISHED SCALES

Diminished scales are octatonic (eight-note) scales separated in sequential whole steps and half steps. There are two types of diminished scales: diminished and inverted diminished.

Diminished scales begin the pattern of whole-step/half-step relationship with a whole step.

Modes of the Diminished Scale

C-E♭-G♭-A diminished	**D♭-E-G-B♭ diminished**	**D-F-A♭-B diminished**
C-D-E♭-F-G♭-A♭-A-B	D♭-E♭-E-G♭-G-A-B♭-C	D-E-F-G-A♭-A-B-C-D♭
E♭-F-G♭-A♭-A-B-C-D	E-F♯-G-A-B♭-C-D♭-E♭	F-G-A♭-B♭-B-C♯-D-E
G♭-A♭-A-B-C-D-E♭-F	G-A-B♭-C-D♭-E♭-E-F♯	A♭-B♭-C♭-D♭-D-E-F-G
A-B-C-D-E♭-F-G♭-A♭	B♭-C-D♭-E♭-E-F♯-G-A	B-C♯-D-E-F-G-A♭-B♭

Inverted Diminished Scales

Inverted diminished scales, also known as half-whole diminished, start with a half step.

Modes of Inverted Diminished Scales

C-E♭-F♯(G♭)-A inverted diminished	**D♭-E-G-B♭ inverted diminished**	**D-F-A♭-B inverted diminished**
C-D♭-E♭-E-F♯-G-A-B♭	D♭-D-E-F-G-A♭-B♭-B	D-E♭-F-G♭-A♭-A-B-C♯
E♭-E-F♯-G-A-B♭-C-D♭	E-F-G-A♭-B♭-B-C♯-D	F-G♭-A♭-A-B-C♯-D-E♭
F♯-G-A-B♭-C-D♭-E♭-E	G-A♭-B♭-B-C♯-D-E-F	A♭-A-B-C♯-D-E♭-F-G♭
A-B♭-C-D♭-E♭-E-F♯-G	B♭-B-C♯-D-E-F-G-A♭	B-C♯-D-E♭-F-G♭-A♭-A

An inverted diminished scale can be applied to any kind of dominant chord. There are other possible applications of diminished scales.

Diminished Scales: Addendum

Diminished scales may also be applied to chords in a manner more specific to the type of chord available.

Possible Scales for Half-Diminished 7th Chords

ø7 or -7(♭5)	-7(♯11)*	Minor Lydian/Mixolydian (4th mode of harmonic minor)
	-7(♭13♭9, ♭5)*	Locrian (7th mode of major)
	-7(♭13, ♭5)*	Diminished/whole-tone (6th mode of melodic minor)
	-7(♭9)**	Dorian ♭2 (2nd mode of melodic minor)
	-7(♭9, ♭5)**	Half-diminished (2nd mode of harmonic minor)
	-7(♭5)**	Dorian ♭5 (2nd mode of harmonic major)

* Generic treatments for subdominant with any type of altered dominant chord.
** Determined by the altered dominant chord especially when tonicizing the I chord.

Benefits of Diminished Scales

Diminished scales, like whole-tone scales, have limited transposition. However, they are one of the most commonly used scales on altered dominant chords, alongside the altered scale and the whole-tone scale.

DIMINISHED SCALES

Applications for Rhythm Changes

Rhythm Changes: Diminished Scale "B" Section

Inverted diminished scales are especially effective on the "B" section, in which scales may have a unison relationship with the chord presented (e.g., D7 = D inverted-diminished).

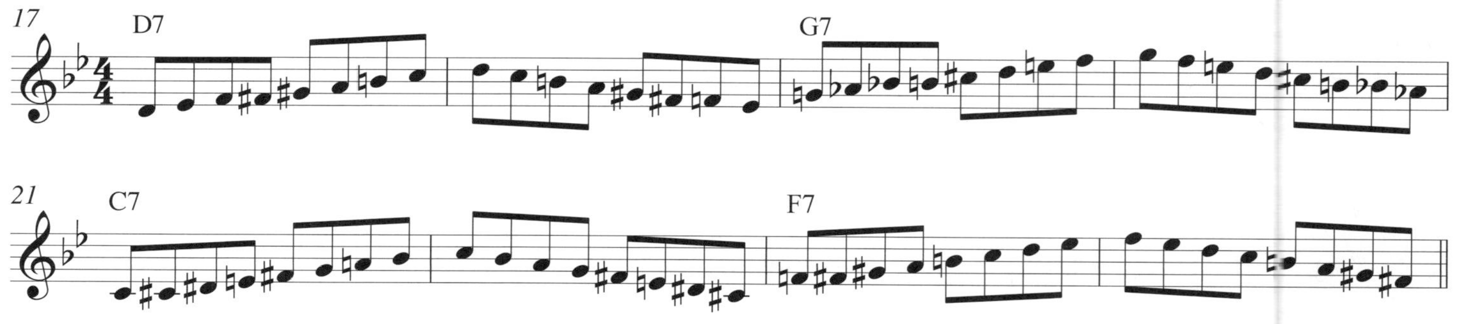

Rhythm Changes: Diminished Scale Example

In the "A" sections, you can apply a diminished scale to the fully diminished 7th chord that appears before the turn around. (e.g., Edim7 = E diminished scale).

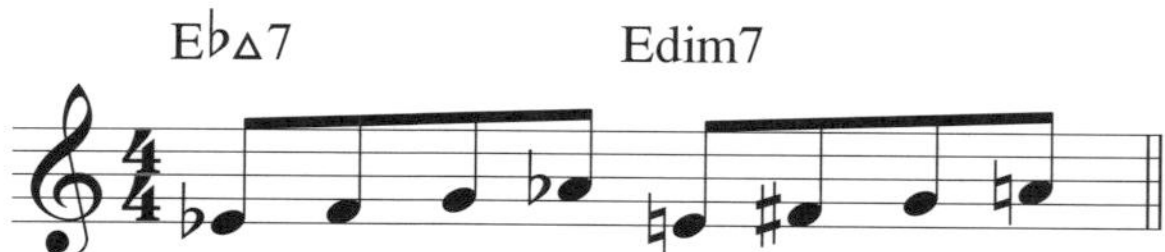

Rhythm Changes: Diminished Scale "A" Section

Both pre-dominant functions and dominant functions may be applied to the half cadences (e.g., F-7–B♭7 = B♭ inverted-diminished).

Avoid applying diminished scales to major 7th chords that are functioning as the tonic.

PLAYING EXERCISES

Practice each etude with a metronome, gradually increasing the tempo over a period of days and weeks. Work toward ♩ = 150.

Rhythm Changes Whole-Tone Scale Study

Rhythm Changes Whole-Tone Scale Study – Retrograde

Rhythm Changes Whole-Tone Scale Study – Alternating (A)

Rhythm Changes Whole-Tone Scale Study – Alternating (B)

Rhythm Changes Diminished Scale Study

Rhythm Changes Diminished Scale Study – Retrograde

Rhythm Changes Diminished Scale Study – Alternating (A)

Rhythm Changes Diminished Scale Study – Alternating (B)

CHAPTER 17
MUSICAL QUOTATION

Concepts, Scales, and Modes

- Musical Quotation

This chapter addresses *musical quotation*. The material here will help you learn how to play short fragments of known melody lines in context, while making the appropriate harmonic alterations that correspond with the chord progression. **Remember:** Do not move on to other exercises until you have mastered each concept. You can do it!

MUSICAL QUOTATION

Musical quotation is the practice of extracting a musical phrase or pattern and applying it in an improvisation. Musical quotations may feature phrases or patterns that come from the same work or may include phrases or patterns appropriated from other sources.

Examples of musical quotation appear in jazz recordings throughout the history of the genre. Charlie Parker, for instance, quoted Stravinsky's *The Rite of Spring* in his solo for "Repetition." Dexter Gordon and Sonny Rollins are especially famed among jazz fans for their use of quotation. A case in point: Rollins, playing alongside Charlie Parker on Miles Davis's *Collector's Items*, throws in a snippet of Irving Berlin's "Anything You Can Do I Can Do Better."

Quotation can enhance the connection between the improviser and the audience, either by paying homage to legendary performances or by creating a sense of nostalgia. For example, the improviser might quote Sonny Rollins or Miles Davis licks, or use a familiar melody as a means to be conversational and communicative. In the case of nostalgic quotations, tunes from the American Songbook (e.g., classic American musicals, jazz standards, Motown standards, classical pops, church hymns, Top 40, etc.) are somewhat familiar and may resonate well with jazz audiences.

BEST PRACTICES

Harmonic Superimposition and "Head" Shifting

When quoting musical phrases in new musical contexts, we need to alter the harmonic structure of the phrase or pattern to fit the current chord progression. Practice this by superimposing a bop-like melody in a new context; for example, play the melody of Charlie Parker's "Donna Lee" over Rhythm Changes. This is most effective if you apply the chord progression of a melody that exists in a key closely related to the bop-like head to be superimposed. (Don't use the same key.) The melody can often be adapted to the new harmonic structure by changing appropriate notes by a half step (usually) or by whole step.

QUOTATION ANYWHERE

Let's examine a blues melody composed by Kris Johnson entitled "Home Grown."

"Home Grown" (Kris Johnson)

Analyze each segment of the melody and categorize the techniques used.

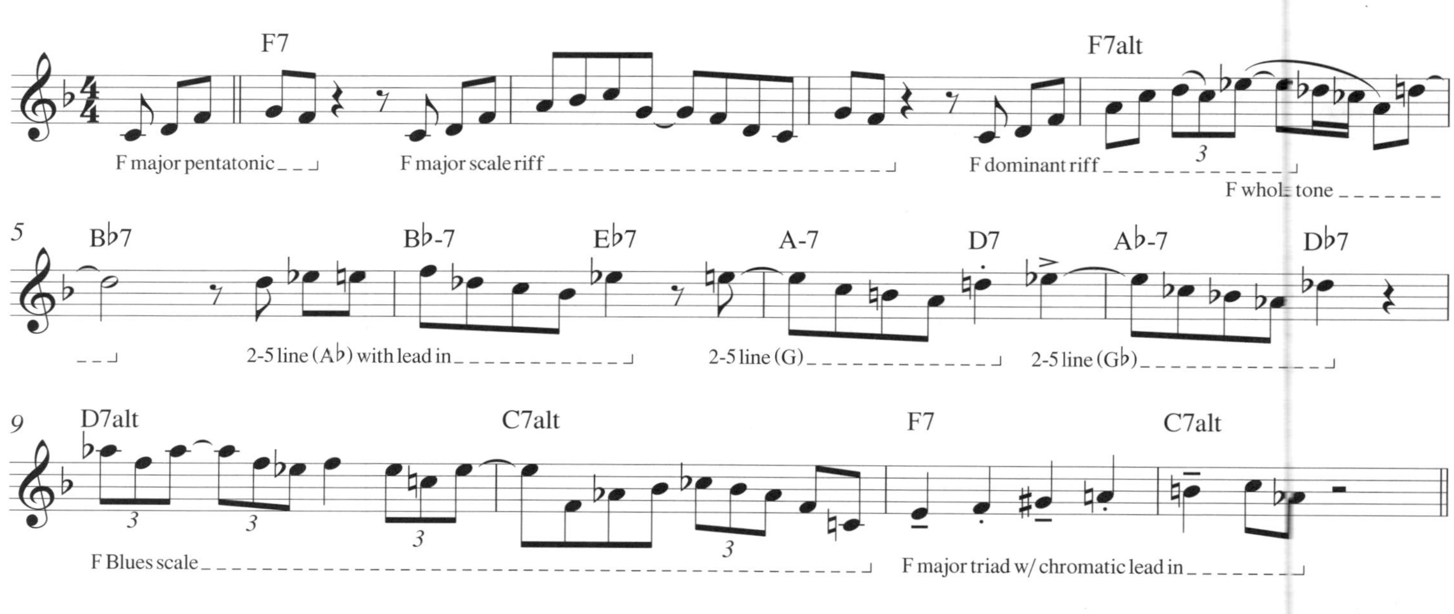

Next, extract the following eight phrases.

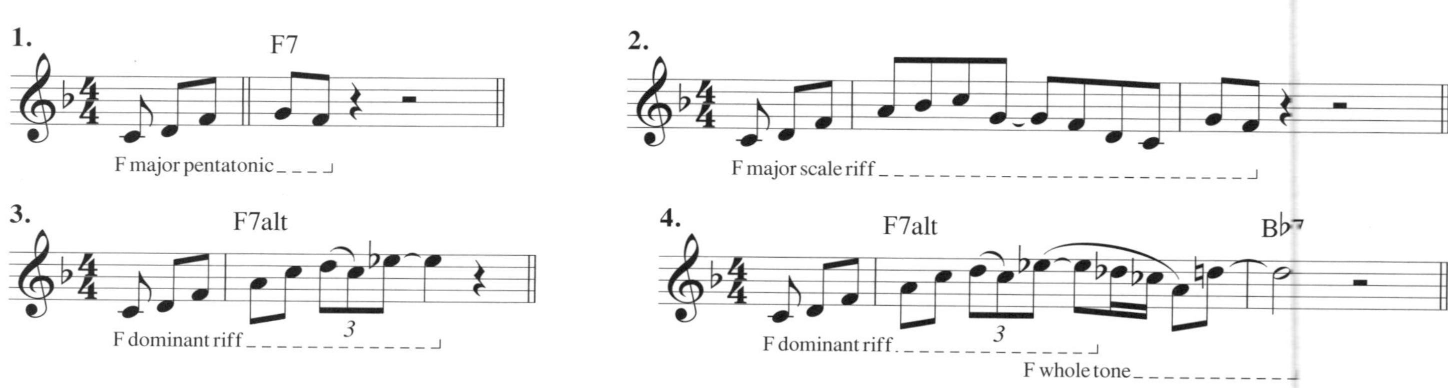

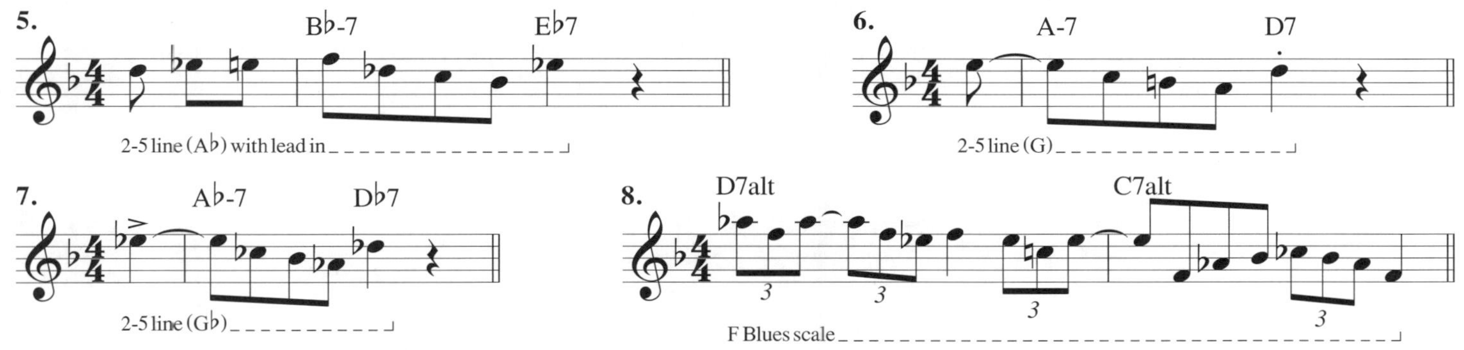

Blues Scale Riff Over the "A" Section of B♭ Rhythm Changes

Imply the phrases over the "A" section of rhythm changes. First, quote a blues scale riff over the "A" section of B♭ rhythm changes.

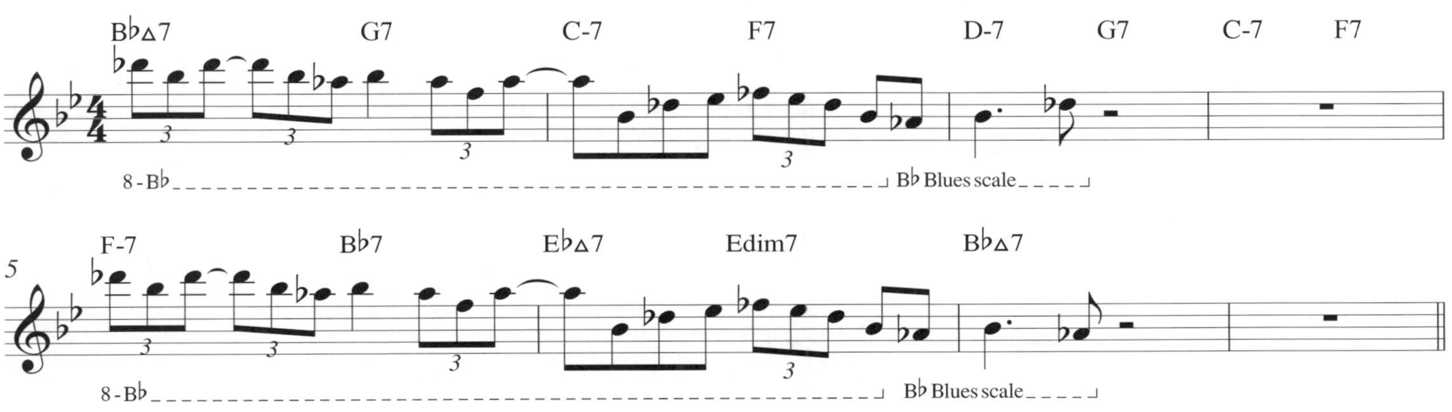

Major Phrase Over the "A" Section of B♭ Rhythm Changes

Render a major phrase over the "A" section of B♭ rhythm changes.

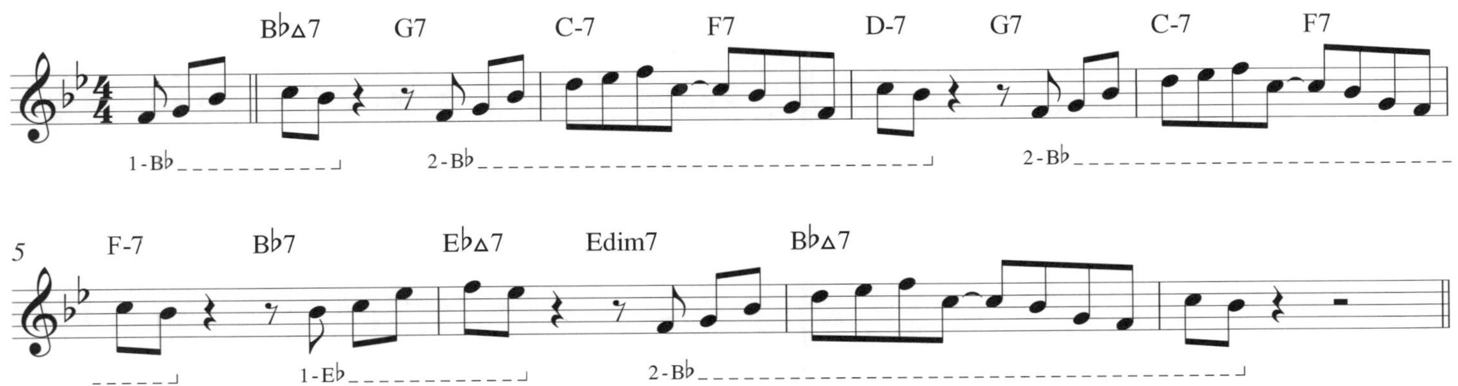

Dominant phrase extracted from "Home Grown": "B" section of B♭ Rhythm Changes

Take the dominant phrase extracted from "Home Grown" and apply it to the "B" section of B♭ rhythm changes.

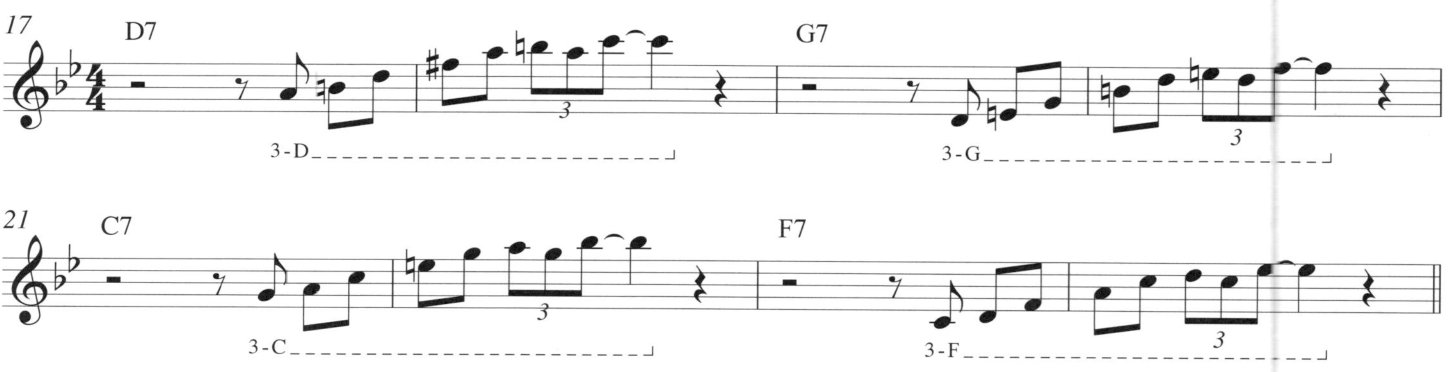

Whole Tone at the End of the Phrase

Extend the previous line by adding the whole-tone run at the end of the phrase and resolve on the subsequent chord.

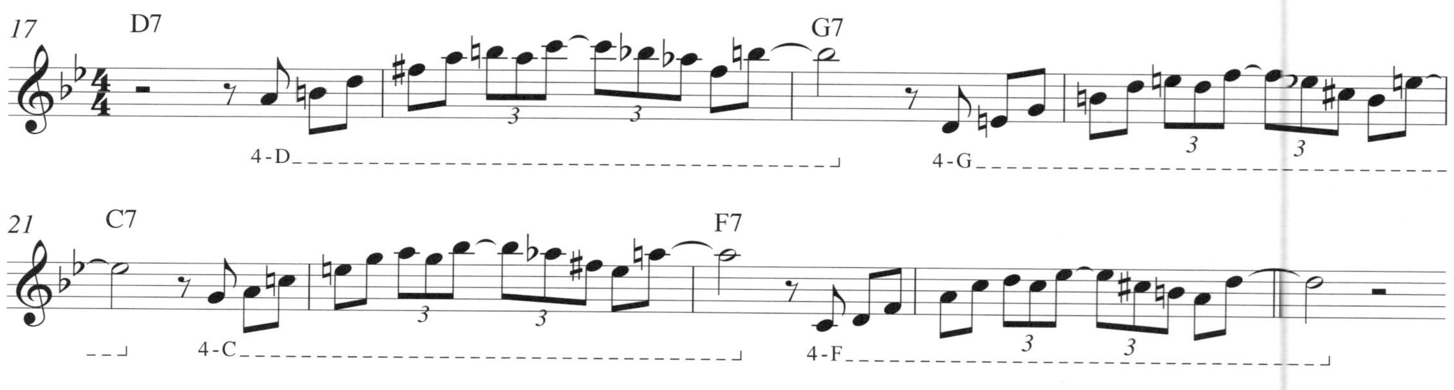

II–V Phrases Implied Using the V Chord

The short II–V phrases taken from "Home Grown" can be implied only using the V chord. Here is an example implied over the "B" section of B♭ rhythm changes.

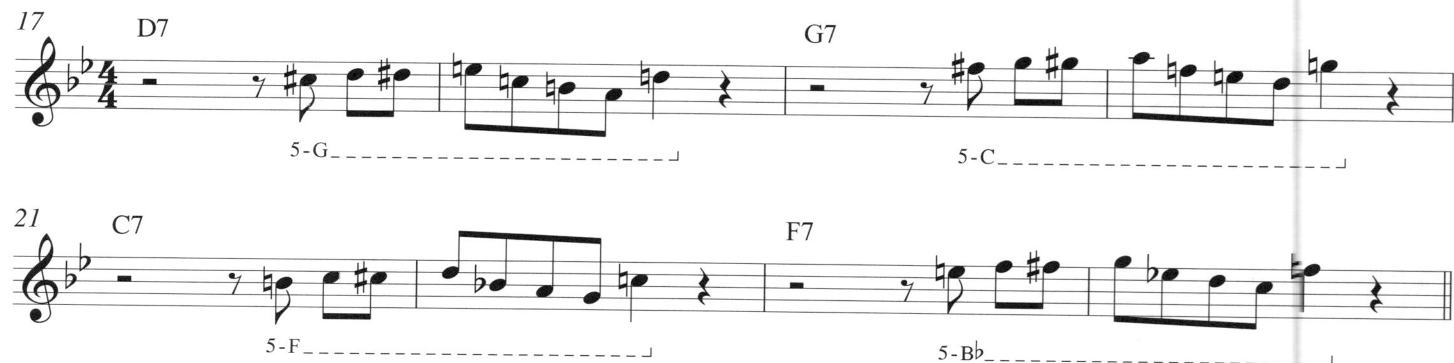

Common Variation: "B" Section of B♭ Rhythm Changes

Below is a common variation of the "B" section of B♭ rhythm changes.

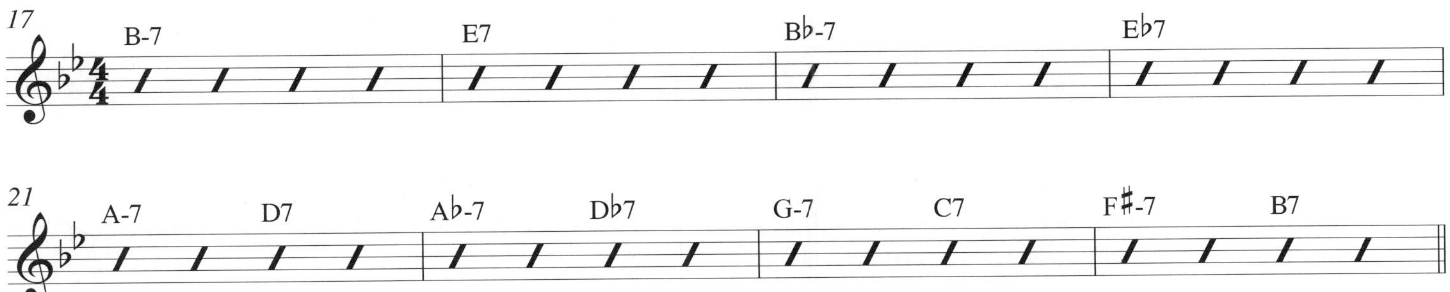

Apply the short II–V phrases to this form.

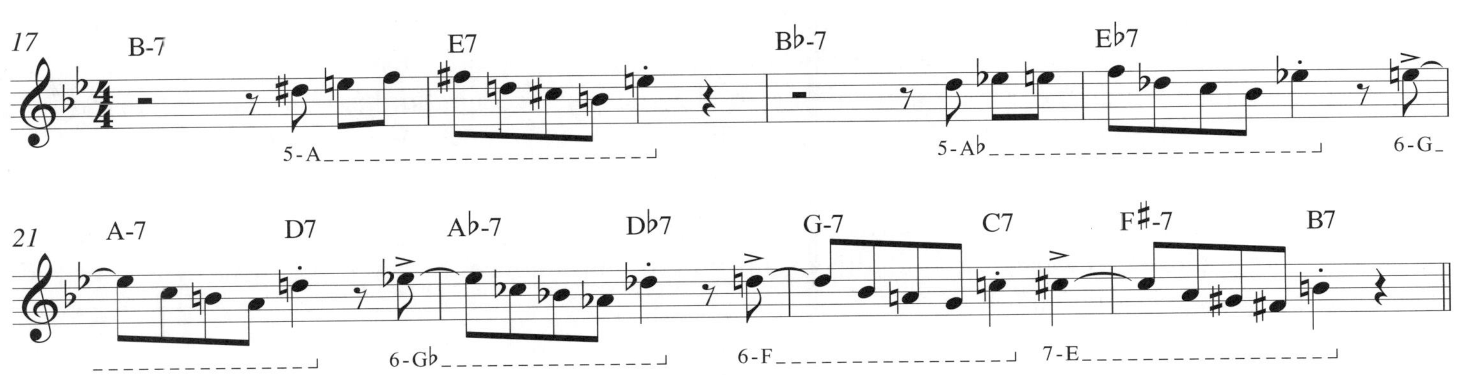

CHAPTER 18
EXERCISES FOR CHALLENGING TUNES

The exercises here contain concepts that have already been explored in previous chapters; by perfecting these etudes, you not only will develop a deeper theoretical understanding of the concepts, but will also acquire increased technical facility and flexibility you can apply to varied concepts within the same harmonic framework.

Each exercise in this chapter is filled with significant rhythmic and harmonic challenges. As always, practice with your trusty metronome, gradually increasing the tempo over a period of days and weeks. Work toward ♩ = 120. You can do it!

Exercise 1: "Angry Winter"
Use this exercise to implement diatonic scales, realized in intervallic jumps, and continuous scale patterns through the composition's chord progression and multiple key centers.

Exercise 2: "Big Foot"
"Big Foot" is characterized by chord changes with unusual root relationships. The roots of the chords are based on the augmented scale, B-D-D♯-F♯-G-B♭-B and so forth. One possible approach for improvisation within the chord progression is to play the first, second, third, and fifth corresponding scale degree of each chord. It allows you a simplified approach to developing facility over the chord changes.

This exercise expounds upon this approach by exploiting positioning of arpeggios in the aforementioned patterns in close relationship to each other. This will, in turn, reduce the perceived distance between the chords and key relationships.

Exercise 3: "Journey"
"Journey" allows you to explore the use of pentatonic and altered pentatonic modes. In application, pentatonic scales may produce a sound that can be perceived both as consonant and as "modern." This exercise will help you expand your understanding of improvised lines, from linear to intervallic, by employing the appropriate pentatonic scale.

Exercise 4: "Pensive"
Due to its long form and unusual key relationship, "Pensive" is ideal for experimentation with shape shifting. Two different shapes are utilized in this exercise: the first shape is shifted over the "A" sections; the second shape is shifted over the bridge. Shape shifting is an important skill for the modern improviser; it will make most improvisations sound mature, thematic, and connected.

Exercise 5: "Sandra by Sunlight"
"Sandra by Starlight" employs a combination of concepts, including – but not limited to – challenging interval patterns, double-time patterns, odd groupings of triplets and septuplets, and chromaticism.

Exercise 6: "Some of the Stuff They Have"
This exercise features bebop triplets (grouped evenly and used to start phrases), bebop accenting, double-time, and whole-tone triad pairs with connecting chromatic passing tones. It's quite a workout, providing you with challenging combinations of rhythmic modulation.

Exercise 7: "Welcome"
"Welcome" uses a variety of harmonic and rhythmic concepts, including – but not limited to – rhythmic displacement and quintuplets.

Exercise 8: "Soulful Life"
"Soulful Life" is comprised primarily of three motives usually associated with a diminished-scale tonality. Those motives are morphed to fit this chord progression. Each chord, with the exception of major 7th chords, is given a diminished-dominant treatment; the shape-shifting exercise becomes an octatonic transposition.

ANGRY WINTER

By Shawn "Thunder" Wallace

BIG FOOT

By Shawn "Thunder" Wallace

JOURNEY

By Shawn "Thunder" Wallace

PENSIVE

By Shawn "Thunder" Wallace

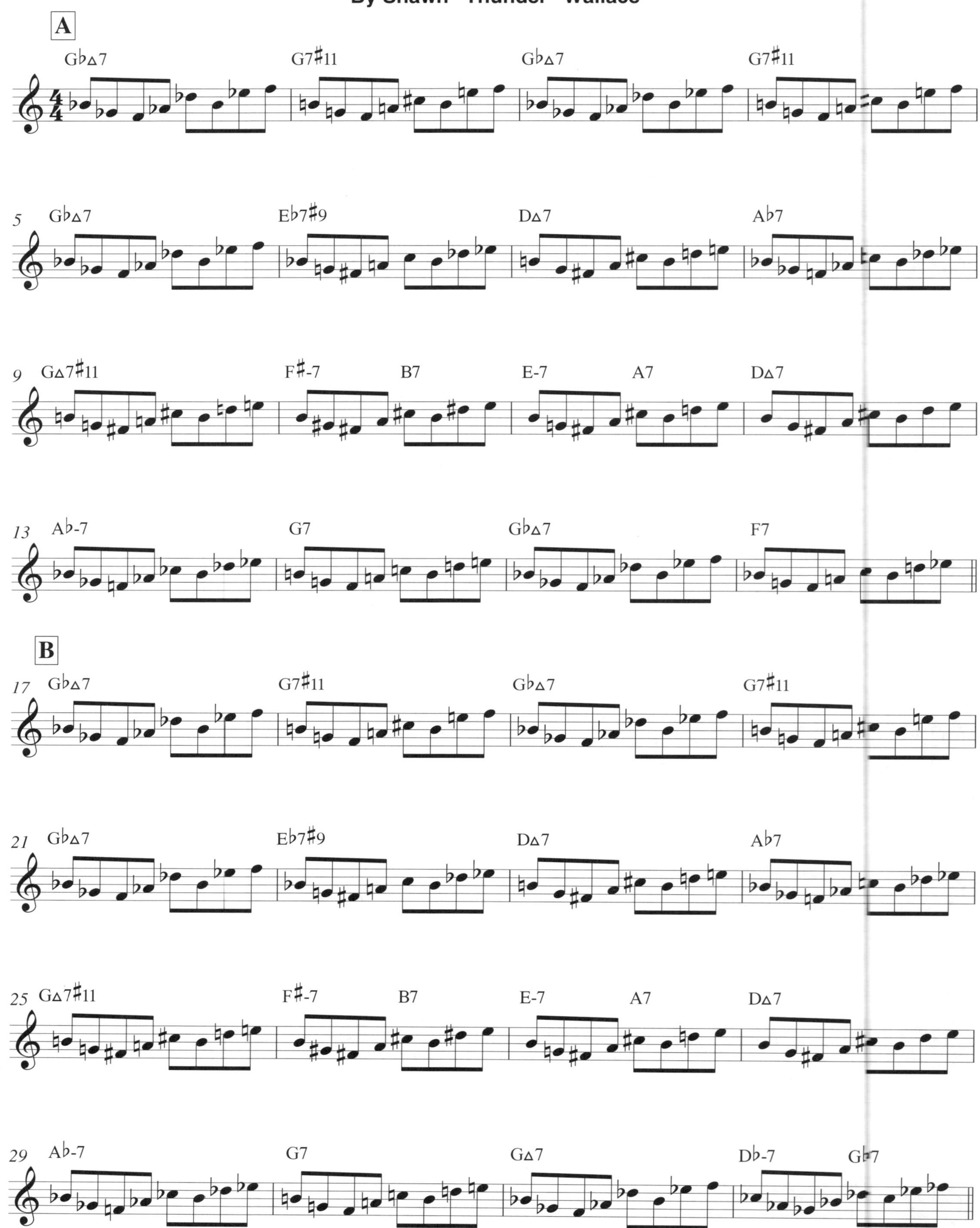

C
33 CΔ7 A-7 FΔ7 E7♯9
37 D-7 G7 CΔ7 B-7 B♭7
41 AΔ7 AΔ7/G♯ F♯-7 B-7 E7♭9
45 AΔ7 D-7 G7
D
49 G♭Δ7 G7♯11 G♭Δ7 G7♯11
53 G♭Δ7 E♭7♯9 DΔ7 DΔ7
57 GΔ7♯11 F♯-7 B7 E-7 A7 DΔ7
61 A♭-7 G7 G♭Δ7 F7

SANDRA BY SUNLIGHT

By Shawn "Thunder" Wallace

SOME OF THE STUFF THEY HAVE

By Shawn "Thunder" Wallace

WELCOME

By Shawn "Thunder" Wallace

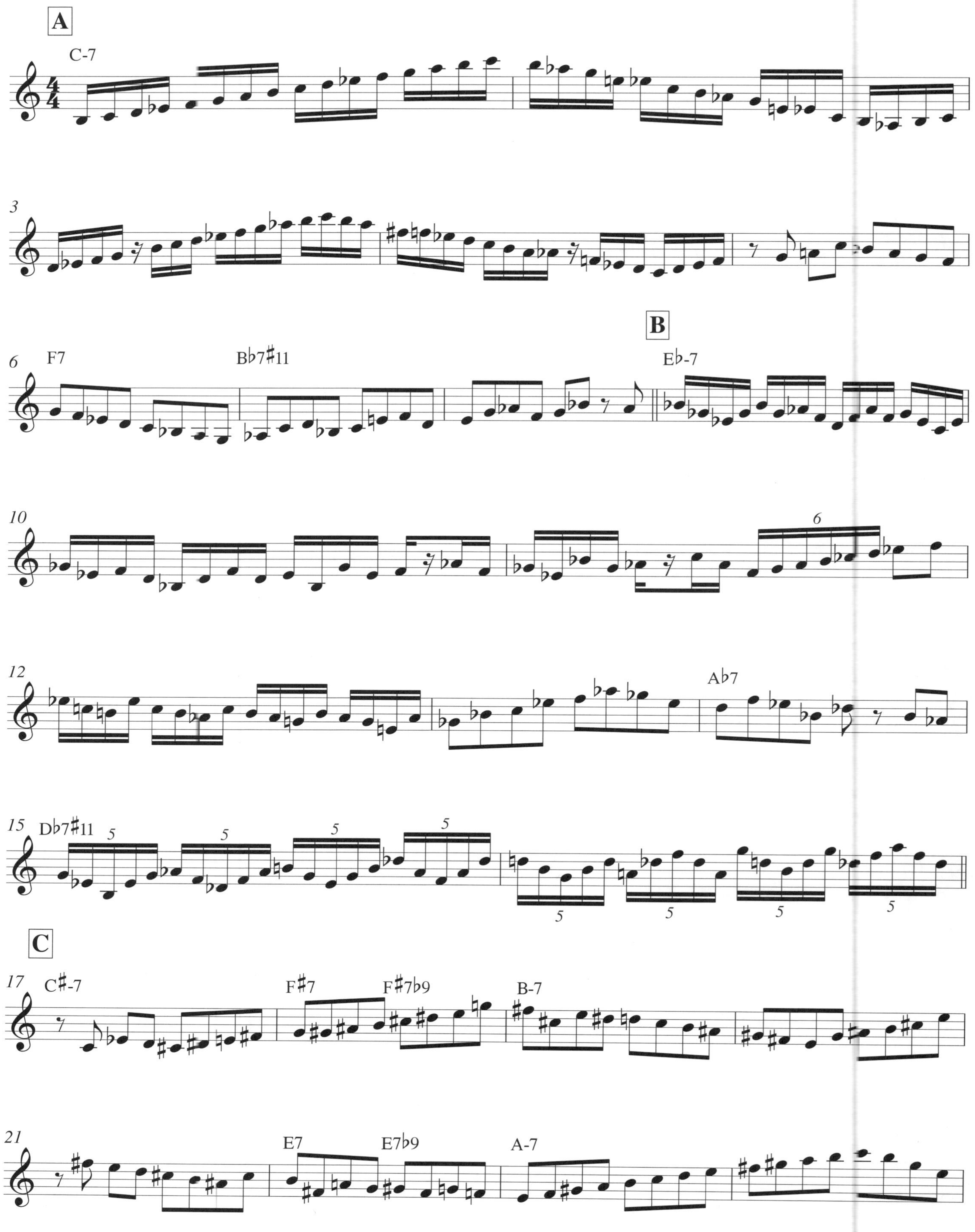

25
A-7
D7
D7♭9
G-7
29
E∅7
E♭7
D7♯9(♯5)
G7♯9(♯5)
D
33
C-7
37
F7
B♭7♯11
41
E♭-7
B7♯5
45
F7♯9(♯5)
B♭7♯9(♯5)
E♭-(△7)

SOULFUL LIFE

By Shawn "Thunder" Wallace

GLOSSARY

accidental: A symbol placed before a note to indicate the raising or lowering of its previously understood pitch. The sharp (♯) raises a note by a half step; the flat (♭) lowers the note by a half step; the natural (♮) cancels a sharp or flat.

altered scale: (a.k.a. inverted diminished/whole-tone scale) The seventh mode of melodic minor. It can be used to play all the alterations of an altered-dominant chord (♯9, ♭9, ♯11, ♯5, ♭5, ♭13).

arpeggio: Playing the notes of a chord in sequence, either ascending or descending, rather than simultaneously. In this text, arpeggios are built using the four most important notes of the chord: root, 3rd, 5th, and 7th.

articulation: Performance techniques that affect changes in the duration of a note. There are various styles of articulation (slurs, phrase marks, staccato, marcato accent, sforzandos, legato, etc.), each of which has a different effect. Articulations can be modified and combined to bring clarity and idiomatic phrasing to the style of music performed.

augmented scale: (a.k.a. symmetrical augmented scale) Constructed of two augmented triads one minor 3rd apart; e.g., C-E-G♯ and E♭-G-B). Enharmonic spelling of notes within augmented scales is common practice. There are three unique augmented scales, each having four modes.

authentic notes: In jazz, these represent certain established conventions found within classic jazz tradition. This typically includes the 3rds and 7ths on any given chord, but can also include 9ths, 11ths, 13ths, and conventional chord alterations (altered 9ths, 5ths, etc.).

bebop accenting: The manner in which bebop players apply rhythmic complexity to phrases by emphasizing certain notes and "ghosting" or "swallowing" other notes. This contrast adds another rhythmic dimension to the improviser's vocabulary.

bebop scale: Scales are derived from the modes of the major scale, the melodic minor scale, and the harmonic minor scale. In general, bebop scales consist of traditional scales with a passing tone strategically placed between whole steps. This text uses four different types of bebop scales: Mixolydian bebop, Dorian bebop, Phyrigian bebop, and Locrian bebop.

Bird blues: A variation of the 12-bar jazz blues in which the structure of Charlie "Bird" Parker's tune "Confirmation" is superimposed over its form. Although "Confirmation" and the Bird blues differ in overall structure, they are similar in that descending ii–V patterns are used to transition smoothly from key center to key center in four-bar increments.

Bird Blues Progression (in F)

| Fmaj7 | Em7♭5 / A7 | Dm7 / G7 | Cm7 / F7 |

| B♭7 | B♭-7 / A♭7 | Am7 / D7 | A♭m7 / D♭7 |

| Gm7 | C7 | Am7 / D7 | Gm7 / C7 |

blue note: In a major scale, the note one half step higher than the fourth degree (♯11) or one half step lower than the fifth degree (♭5). In the key of C major, for example, this note would be F♯/G♭. The blue note is used for expressivity within the blues.

blues: As a form, the blues can be identified by its specific chord progression; the traditional 12-bar blues is perhaps the most common. It also is recognizable (both in genre and in form) through the use of blue notes, certain scale degrees that, for expressive purposes, are altered, bent, or modified.

blues scale: A six-note scale that combines the minor pentatonic scale with the blue note. It is constructed of root, minor 3rd, 4th, ♭5th, ♮5th, and ♭7th. For example, the B♭ blues scale is spelled B♭-D♭-E♭-E-F-A♭; here, the "blue note" is E.

canvas approach: A method of improvisation in which the player is limited to using a single stylistic or conceptual constraint (e.g., a scale or mode) for improvisation. This can be implemented in a number of ways – for a section of a piece or even for an entire song, if desired.

chord: The simultaneous sounding of two or more notes. Dyad: two notes; triad: three notes; tetrad: four notes.

chord progression: (or harmonic progression) A sequence of chords that aims for the specific goal of establishing – or contradicting – a given tonality (key, root, or tonic).

chord-scale theory: A method of matching chords and scales within jazz harmony. It has been widely used since the 1970s and is generally accepted in the jazz world today. Examples in this text are based largely on chord-scale theory as it is applied to jazz harmony.

chromaticism: A technique whereby the primary diatonic pitches and chords of a given key are interspersed with other pitches of the chromatic scale. These pitches, which are outside the stated tonality, are resolved via half step to notes within the diatonic scale.

church modes: The seven diatonic modes originating from a major scale:

- **Ionian:** (maj7)
- **Dorian:** (m7)
- **Phyrigian:** (m7♭13(♭9))
- **Lydian:** (maj7(♯11))
- **Mixolydian:** (7)
- **Aolean:** (m7♭13)
- **Locrian:** (m7♭13(♭9, ♭5))

continuous scale: The practice of applying stepwise motion across an entire chord progression. This practice removes wider intervals from the improvisation and forces the improviser to develop linear ideas.

diatonic: Based on an octave divided into five whole steps and two half steps. The major scale, the natural minor scale, and the church modes are diatonic. Chords and intervals derived from diatonic scales are said to have diatonic relationships.

diminished scale: Octatonic (eight-note) scales comprised of sequential whole and half steps. There are two types of diminished scales: diminished and inverted diminished. Diminished scales begin the pattern of whole-step/half-step relationship with a whole step. Three distinct diminished scales (with the same sequence of intervals) can be created by starting at a different point within the scale. For example:

- E♭ diminished (F♯/G♭, A, C diminished): E♭-F-F♯-G♯-A-B-C-D-E♭
- D diminished (F, A♭, B diminished): D-E-F-G-A♭-B♭-B-C♯-D
- D♭ diminished (E, G, B♭ diminished): D♭-E♭-E-F♯-G-A-B♭-C-D♭

dominant 7th chords: A chord consisting of a root, major 3rd, perfect 5th, and minor 7th (or a major triad with a minor 7th). Technically, it occurs on the fifth scale degree (dominant), but in the blues its sonority is also used for tonic and subdominant functions.

Dorian scale: The second of the eight traditional church modes; it is the second mode of the major scale. It can be used to play on the minor chord in a major ii–V pattern, but also can be used to tonicize a minor I chord.

dynamics: The aspect of musical expression resulting from variation in the volume of sound. Standard dynamic marks used in music are

pp: pianissimo; very soft

p: piano; soft

mp: mezzo piano; moderately soft

mf: mezzo forte; moderately loud

f: forte; loud

ff: fortissimo; very loud

eighth-note phrasing: A type of phrasing particular to the emphasis of an eighth note on or off the beat. There are three basic types.

- **Prebop (1920s-1940s):** Notes are swung, with emphasis placed on the beat (the first part of the triplet).
- **Bebop (1940s-late 1950s):** Notes are swung, but emphasis is placed on the "and" of the beat (approx. the last eighth note of the triplet).
- **Postbop (1960s and beyond):** Notes are almost even in value, with emphasis placed on the "and" of the beat and notes are played evenly.

enclosure: A form of chromaticism in which a target note in the upcoming chord is preceded by (or enclosed by) other notes. Enclosure is used to emphasize or delay a particular resolution.

fully-diminished 7th Chords (dim7): Chords constructed of stacked minor 3rds. In the blues, a diminished 7th chord is used as a transitional chord.

flat: A notational sign (♭) indicating that the note is to be lowered in pitch by a half step (semitone).

ghost notes: Notes that are deemphasized (ghosted), often to the point of near silence, within a musical phrase.

half step: (or semitone) The smallest interval in Western music;, e.g., C-C♯ or C-D♭.

half-diminished 7th chord (ø7): A diminished triad with a minor 7th. A half-diminished 7th chord made up of a root, a minor 3rd, a tritone, and a minor 7th. It is most commonly found in the blues as a transitional chord, and serves a subdominant (IV) function.

half-step relationships: An approach to improvisation that frees the player from having to start or continue a pattern from the root of the chord. The bias inherent to root relationships is avoided and the amount of material that can be played in a specific range is maximized, facilitating the connection of patterns using the smallest interval available.

harmonic major scale: A major scale with lowered 6th (♭13); it offers a canvas approach to an altered ii–V pattern that resolves to a major I in which the harmonic function of the progression supersedes the dissonance produced by the lowered 6th (♭13).

harmonic minor scale: Constructed using a lowered 3rd, lowered 6th, and raised 7th; the raised 7th is in accordance with the major triad on the fifth scale degree (V), which provides another option to tonicize a minor I chord.

harmonic progression: See chord progression.

hemiola: In modern musical practice, the articulation of two bars of triple time (e.g., 3/4) as if they were three bars in duple time (e.g., 2/4). Hemiola can be applied to repeated rhythmic patterns that are outside of the stress of the established pulse, causing the sensation of displacement.

hexatonic scale and six-note scale intervals: A symmetrical scale constructed from the combination of two augmented triads minor 3rd (or augmented 2nd) apart.

inverted augmented scale: Constructed of two augmented triads placed one half step apart (e.g., C-E-G♯ and D♭-F-A). Inverted augmented scales begin their pattern with a half step. Enharmonic spelling of notes within inverted augmented scales is common practice. There are three unique inverted augmented scales, each having four modes.

inverted diminished scale: An eight-note scale built from alternating whole steps and half steps, starting with a half step. For example, a C inverted diminished scale = C-D♭-E♭-E-F♯-G-A-B♭.

leading tone: In Western music theory, the seventh scale degree of the diatonic scale that leads melodically to the tonic of the home key. The leading tone resolves ("leads") to another note one semitone higher or lower, being a lower and upper leading tone, respectively.

major 7th chords: A major triad with a major 3rd on top; a major 7th chord has a root, major 3rd, perfect 5th, and major 7th. It is the chord most commonly used for tonic functions.

major pentatonic scale: A five-note scale created by using the first, second, fourth, fifth, and sixth scale degrees of the natural minor scale. In the key of B♭ major, for example, this scale would consist of the notes B♭(1)-C(2)-E(4)-F(5)-G(6).

melodic minor scale: In its ascending form, the 3rd is lowered, while the sixth and seventh scale degrees are raised. In its descending form, the scale is identical to natural minor. In jazz, the melodic minor scale is the same ascending and descending. It retains the lowered 3rd, natural 6th, and natural 7th in both the ascending and descending forms.

metric modulation: To superimpose or aurally infer a different meter grouping than what is being played. For example, playing triplets in two-note or four-note groupings instead of three-note groupings implies compound time (2 over 3, 3 over 4).

metronome: A device used to establish an appropriate tempo for a piece and to help maintain consistency of tempo throughout.

minor 7th chords: A minor triad with a minor 7th; a minor 7th chord has a root, minor 3rd, perfect 5th, and minor 7th. It is most commonly found in the blues, in ii–V chord progressions, and serves a subdominant (IV) function.

minor blues: A tune in a minor key that follows the standard chord progression of a 12-bar blues; the chord progression and improvisation are altered to fit the styles used within classic jazz. A typical minor blues may follow a chord progression similar to the one shown below:

| B♭m7 | E♭m7 | B♭m7 | B♭7 |

| E♭7m | E♭7m | B♭7 | Dm7 / G7 |

| Cm7 | F7 | B♭m7 | Cm7 / F7 |

minor pentatonic scale: A five-note scale created by using the first, third, fourth, fifth, and seventh scale degree of the natural minor scale. In the key of B♭ minor, for example, this scale would be spelled B♭(1)-D♭(3)-E♭(4)-F(5)-A♭(7).

modes: Sometimes called "church modes," these are the categories into which Gregorian chant was classified from about the ninth century. There are seven modes that can be derived from a major scale:

- **Ionian:** maj7
- **Dorian:** m7
- **Phrygian:** m7 (♭13, ♭9)
- **Lydian:** maj7 (♯11)
- **Mixolydian:** 7
- **Aeolian:** m7 (♭13)
- **Locrian:** m7 (♭13, ♭9, ♭5)

natural minor scale: The sixth mode (Aeolian) of the major scale; natural minor can be used to tonicize a minor I chord, similar to Dorian. Although it has been a long-standing practice in jazz to use Dorian to tonicize the minor I, from a functional perspective, natural minor is a more accurate choice.

octatonic scale: Any eight-note scale, usually occurring within the confines of an octave.

pentatonic scale: Can refer to any five-note scale within an octave, but more commonly denotes the major pentatonic scale.

phraseology: Communicating the fixed expressions, musical idioms, and stock phrases found in a particular musical genre.

root relationships: Building patterns from the roots of chords in a given progression. This allows the improviser to explore the sound of each chord from the foundation of the harmony.

Rhythm Changes: Jazz term for the chord progression of George Gershwin's song "I Got Rhythm."

scale: A collection of notes arranged in ascending and/or descending order. A scale is long enough to explicitly define a mode or tonality; it begins or ends on the fundamental note (tonic) of that mode or tonality.

semitone: See half step.

seventh chord (7th chord): A chord constructed of a triad plus a 7th above the chord's root. There are many several types of 7th chords, including – but not limited to – a chord constructed of a root, major 7th, minor 7th, dominant 7th, diminished 7th, half-diminished 7th, augmented 7th, minor/major 7th.

sharp: A notational sign (♯) indicating that the note is to be raised in pitch by a half step (semitone).

tempo: The speed or pace of a musical composition.

tertian: Describes a chord constructed from the interval of a 3rd. For example, an A major triad is constructed of two intervals: one major 3rd (A-C♯) and one minor 3rd (C♯-E).

thirds (3rds) and sevenths (7ths): 3rd and the 7ths are those notes which help to define the quality of the 7th chord and provide foundation points around which improvisers may shape melodic and/or rhythmic structures.

triad pairs: Any two triads with no notes in common. Triad pairs are an effective way to incorporate larger intervals into solos while also specifically defining two separate constructs (bitonality). Triad pairs can serve as a basis to form melodic and intervallic patterns using hexatonic (six-note) structures.

unison relationships: Chords and scales are compared to each other based on their common root (usually starting with the major key); e.g., C major, C minor, C Lydian, etc.

whole step: (or whole tone) The interval equal to the sum of two half steps (two semitones).

whole-tone scale: Hexatonic (six-note) scale in which each note is separated from its neighbors by one whole step. Enharmonic spelling of notes within whole-tone scales is common practice. There are two unique whole-tone scales, each scale having six modes.

ACKNOWLEDGMENTS

Thanks to Dr. Keith Newton, Kris Johnson, and Steve Kortyka for their assistance in completing this book. Keith, thanks so much for your "Primer" chapter, for keeping us on task, and for your special attention to the narrative. Kris, thanks for your excellent engraving work, for collaboration and input throughout the book – especially Riff-Based Improvisation and Quotation – and for the clarity through the exercises. Steve, thanks for your significant collaboration not only on Triad Pairs, but also on fleshing out of many of the initial exercises, as well as keeping us moving forward with your many "hit list" emails.

I'd like to thank Dr. Ted McDaniel for hiring me at The Ohio State University; the experience of teaching gave me the opportunity to refine many of the concepts in this book. I'd also like to thank my wife, Lorii A. Wallace. She has been most supportive; when progress was lagging, she often gave me a gentle nudge to get back to work. I'd like to thank my father, Mickey Wallace. If it weren't for him, I wouldn't even be a musician. I hope I can be half the father he has been to me. I'd like to thank my mother, Phyllis Wallace, who imparted to me a strong since of spirituality. And I'd be remiss if I didn't thank my Heavenly Father above... Lord Jesus Christ, Son of God, have mercy on me, a sinner! Thank You for the gift of music and for Your new mercies each morning!

– Shawn "Thunder" Wallace

I would like to thank my colleagues Shawn "Thunder" Wallace, Kris Johnson, and Steven Kortyka for graciously sharing their expertise and knowledge to create this text. Gentlemen, your skills as musicians and educators is substantive; my experience in creating this text with you has been one from which I have benefited not only because of your commitment to excellence, but also because of your desire to help others learn and grow. Thank you for helping to make this project successful.

– Dr. Keith Newton

I'm honored to serve as an author and engraver for *How To Improvise Over Chord Changes*. Major thanks to Shawn, Keith, and Steven for inviting me to contribute to this project. I appreciate your thoroughness and passion for education.

– Kris Johnson

I would like to extend a heartfelt "thank you" to Shawn, Keith, and Kris for continuing to include me as part of this project even though I wasn't able be there for its entirety. I am truly humbled and honored to have my name among three such hard-working and talented individuals who are consistently augmenting both jazz and jazz education.

– Steven Kortyka

ABOUT THE AUTHORS

Shawn "Thunder" Wallace

Shawn "Thunder" Wallace is a talented performer, recording artist, composer, clinician, and educator, skilled in jazz music and equally comfortable with classical, contemporary Christian, and gospel music. He has been seen and heard nationally on CBS, BET, NBC, and NPR, and appeared in the film *Miles Ahead* (2015). In addition to receiving recognition from many newspapers and publications, including *Billboard* and *Contemporary Christian Music* magazine, he is a winner of *Downbeat* magazine's outstanding soloist award.

Wallace is the Director of Jazz Studies and Associate Professor of Jazz Saxophone at The Ohio State University. He is also the Creative Director at Vineyard Columbus. He has released eight CDs, is a multi-instrumentalist (saxophone, flute, clarinet, piano, bass, and guitar) and is the leader of Perfect Storm and the Shawn "Thunder" Wallace Quartet. Thunder is a Vandoren Artist and endorses Gemeinhardt Musical Instruments, and is pursuing a DMA in Saxophone Performance at the University of Cincinnati (CCM).

Dr. Keith Newton

Dr. Keith Newton is a multifaceted performer, educator, and creator of media. His specialization is the cross-disciplinary integration of musical works and visual arts through computer technology. The combination of live music and technology can be experienced in his many performances with studio productions with established and emerging artists. Newton is also an established web developer with expertise in Web Accessibility, development and implementation of interactive training, and the production of audiovisual media for distribution upon multiple platforms.

Keith holds a Bachelor of Science degree in Music Education from Capital University. He received his Master of Music and Doctor of Musical Arts degrees from The Ohio State University.

Kris Johnson

Kris Johnson is an award-winning jazz trumpeter, composer, and educator. He has appeared on an impressive list of albums, including two Grammy-nominated releases: Tony Bennett's *A Swingin' Christmas* and Karen Clark Sheard's *All in One*. Kris is a trumpeter and arranger with the Count Basie Orchestra. In 2013, he was featured in the standup-comedy film *Make Me Wanna Holla*, starring Sinbad.

Drawing from jazz, classical, hip-hop, and neo-soul, Kris's writing creates diverse textures that represent his unique musical identity. He has composed several large-scale works for jazz and orchestral ensembles, including *Jim Crow's Tears* (musical for six ensemble members and a jazz orchestra), *A Journey Through a Dream* (jazz ensemble and string quartet commissioned by the Arts League of Michigan), and *Odd Expressions* (jazz ensemble and symphony orchestra commissioned by Troy High School). His arrangements have been performed and/or recorded by the Count Basie Orchestra, Karen Clark Sheard, Yolanda Adams, the Clark Sisters, Farmington Community Band, the Motor City Brass Band, Detroit Symphony's Civic Jazz Ensembles, and many others. He is also the exclusive copyist for composer and trombonist Wycliffe Gordon.

Currently, Kris Johnson is the Director of Jazz Studies at the University of Utah. Kris holds master's and bachelor's degrees in Jazz Studies from Michigan State University. In 2012, Kris received an ASCAP Herb Alpert Young Jazz Composers award and was selected as one of 25 Detroit performing and literary artists to receive a Kresge Artist Fellowship.

Steven Korytka

Steven Kortyka is a full time multi-instrumentalist, composer, and educator residing in Astoria, New York. In addition to being a soloist and arranger on the Grammy Award-winning album *Cheek to Cheek* (featuring Lady Gaga and Tony Bennett), he has had the opportunity to share the stage with a number of notable legends, including Frank Sinatra Jr., the Temptations featuring Dennis Edwards, Megan Hilty, Jim Belushi, Lady Gaga, and Count Basie's favorite drummer, Harold Jones. Steve has made national appearances on *Cheek to Cheek: Live, A Very Gaga Thanksgiving*, *The Jimmy Fallon Show*, *Strictly Come Dancing* (UK), *Christmas at Rockefeller Center*, *NYE with Carson Daly*, and *Good Morning America.*

Upon receiving his Bachelor's Degree in Performance and Education from the University of Cincinnati in 2004, he joined cruise ships, where he was promoted to Musical Director after a year. Since moving to New York City, Steve has been interviewed in numerous online publications, including *PMC* magazine, *CityBeat*, and *Saxophone Today* and frequently appears as a clinician and/or private instructor across the country. For more info, visit www.stevekortyka.com.

Presenting the Hal Leonard JAZZ PLAY-ALONG® SERIES

For use with all B-flat, E-flat, Bass Clef and C instruments, the Jazz Play-Along® Series is the ultimate learning tool for all jazz musicians. With musician-friendly lead sheets, melody cues, and other split-track audio choices included, these first-of-a-kind packages help you master improvisation while playing some of the greatest tunes of all time. FOR STUDY, each tune includes a split track with: melody cue with proper style and inflection • professional rhythm tracks • choruses for soloing • removable bass part • removable piano part. FOR PERFORMANCE, each tune also has: an additional full stereo accompaniment track (no melody) • additional choruses for soloing.

1A. MAIDEN VOYAGE/ALL BLUES
00843158 .... $15.99

1. DUKE ELLINGTON
00841644........ $16.99

2. MILES DAVIS
00841645........ $16.99

3. THE BLUES
00841646........ $16.99

4. JAZZ BALLADS
00841691........ $16.99

5. BEST OF BEBOP
00841689........ $16.99

6. JAZZ CLASSICS WITH EASY CHANGES
00841690........ $16.99

7. ESSENTIAL JAZZ STANDARDS
00843000........ $16.99

8. ANTONIO CARLOS JOBIM AND THE ART OF THE BOSSA NOVA
00843001........ $16.99

9. DIZZY GILLESPIE
00843002........ $16.99

10. DISNEY CLASSICS
00843003........ $16.99

12. ESSENTIAL JAZZ CLASSICS
00843005........ $16.99

13. JOHN COLTRANE
00843006........ $16.99

14. IRVING BERLIN
00843007........ $16.99

15. RODGERS & HAMMERSTEIN
00843008........ $16.99

16. COLE PORTER
00843009........ $16.99

17. COUNT BASIE
00843010........ $16.99

18. HAROLD ARLEN
00843011........ $16.99

20. CHRISTMAS CAROLS
00843080........ $16.99

21. RODGERS AND HART CLASSICS
00843014........ $16.99

22. WAYNE SHORTER
00843015........ $16.99

23. LATIN JAZZ
00843016........ $16.99

24. EARLY JAZZ STANDARDS
00843017........ $16.99

25. CHRISTMAS JAZZ
00843018........ $16.99

26. CHARLIE PARKER
00843019........ $16.99

27. GREAT JAZZ STANDARDS
00843020........ $16.99

28. BIG BAND ERA
00843021........ $16.99

29. LENNON AND MCCARTNEY
00843022........ $16.99

30. BLUES' BEST
00843023........ $16.99

31. JAZZ IN THREE
00843024........ $16.99

32. BEST OF SWING
00843025........ $17.99

33. SONNY ROLLINS
00843029........ $16.99

34. ALL TIME STANDARDS
00843030........ $16.99

35. BLUESY JAZZ
00843031........ $16.99

36. HORACE SILVER
00843032........ $16.99

37. BILL EVANS
00843033........ $16.99

38. YULETIDE JAZZ
00843034........ $16.99

39. "ALL THE THINGS YOU ARE" & MORE JEROME KERN SONGS
00843035........ $16.99

40. BOSSA NOVA
00843036........ $16.99

41. CLASSIC DUKE ELLINGTON
00843037........ $16.99

42. GERRY MULLIGAN FAVORITES
00843038........ $16.99

43. GERRY MULLIGAN CLASSICS
00843039........ $16.99

45. GEORGE GERSHWIN
00103643........ $24.99

47. CLASSIC JAZZ BALLADS
00843043........ $16.99

48. BEBOP CLASSICS
00843044........ $16.99

49. MILES DAVIS STANDARDS
00843045........ $16.99

52. STEVIE WONDER
00843048........ $16.99

53. RHYTHM CHANGES
00843049........ $16.99

55. BENNY GOLSON
00843052........ $16.99

56. "GEORGIA ON MY MIND" & OTHER SONGS BY HOAGY CARMICHAEL
00843056........ $16.99

57. VINCE GUARALDI
00843057........ $16.99

58. MORE LENNON AND MCCARTNEY
00843059........ $16.99

59. SOUL JAZZ
00843060........ $16.99

60. DEXTER GORDON
00843061........ $16.99

61. MONGO SANTAMARIA
00843062........ $16.99

62. JAZZ-ROCK FUSION
00843063........ $16.99

63. CLASSICAL JAZZ
00843064........ $16.99

64. TV TUNES
00843065........ $16.99

65. SMOOTH JAZZ
00843066........ $16.99

66. A CHARLIE BROWN CHRISTMAS
00843067........ $16.99

67. CHICK COREA
00843068........ $16.99

68. CHARLES MINGUS
00843069........ $16.99

71. COLE PORTER CLASSICS
00843073........ $16.99

72. CLASSIC JAZZ BALLADS
00843074........ $16.99

73. JAZZ/BLUES
00843075........ $16.99

74. BEST JAZZ CLASSICS
00843076........ $16.99

75. PAUL DESMOND
00843077........ $16.99

78. STEELY DAN
00843070........ $16.99

79. MILES DAVIS CLASSICS
00843081........ $16.99

80. JIMI HENDRIX
00843083........ $16.99

83. ANDREW LLOYD WEBBER
00843104........ $16.99

84. BOSSA NOVA CLASSICS
00843105........ $16.99

85. MOTOWN HITS
00843109........ $16.99

86. BENNY GOODMAN
00843110........ $16.99

87. DIXIELAND
00843111........ $16.99

90. THELONIOUS MONK CLASSICS
00841262 .... $16.99

91. THELONIOUS MONK FAVORITES
00841263 .... $16.99

92. LEONARD BERNSTEIN
00450134 .... $16.99

93. DISNEY FAVORITES
00843142 .... $16.99

94. RAY
00843143 .... $16.99

95. JAZZ AT THE LOUNGE
00843144 .... $16.99

96. LATIN JAZZ STANDARDS
00843145 .... $16.99

97. MAYBE I'M AMAZED*
00843148 .... $16.99

98. DAVE FRISHBERG
00843149 .... $16.99

99. SWINGING STANDARDS
00843150 .... $16.99

100. LOUIS ARMSTRONG
00740423 .... $16.99

101. BUD POWELL
00843152 .... $16.99

102. JAZZ POP
00843153 .... $16.99

103. ON GREEN DOLPHIN STREET & OTHER JAZZ CLASSICS
00843154 .... $16.99

104. ELTON JOHN
00843155 .... $16.99

105. SOULFUL JAZZ
00843151 .... $16.99

106. SLO' JAZZ
00843117 .... $16.99

107. MOTOWN CLASSICS
00843116 .... $16.99

108. JAZZ WALTZ
00843159 .... $16.99

109. OSCAR PETERSON
00843160 .... $16.99

110. JUST STANDARDS
00843161 .... $16.99

111. COOL CHRISTMAS
00843162 .... $16.99

112. PAQUITO D'RIVERA – LATIN JAZZ*
48020662 .... $16.99

113. PAQUITO D'RIVERA – BRAZILIAN JAZZ*
48020663 .... $19.99

114. MODERN JAZZ QUARTET FAVORITES
00843163 .... $16.99

115. THE SOUND OF MUSIC
00843164 .... $16.99

116. JACO PASTORIUS
00843165 .... $16.99

117. ANTONIO CARLOS JOBIM – MORE HITS
00843166 .... $16.99

118. BIG JAZZ STANDARDS COLLECTION
00843167 .... $27.50

119. JELLY ROLL MORTON
00843168 .... $16.99

120. J.S. BACH
00843169 .... $16.99

121. DJANGO REINHARDT
00843170 .... $16.99

122. PAUL SIMON
00843182 .... $16.99

123. BACHARACH & DAVID
00843185 .... $16.99

124. JAZZ-ROCK HORN HITS
00843186 .... $16.99

125. SAMMY NESTICO
00843187 .... $16.99

126. COUNT BASIE CLASSICS
00843157 .... $16.99

127. CHUCK MANGIONE
00843188 .... $16.99

128. VOCAL STANDARDS (LOW VOICE)
00843189 .... $16.99

129. VOCAL STANDARDS (HIGH VOICE)
00843190 .... $16.99

130. VOCAL JAZZ (LOW VOICE)
00843191 .... $16.99

131. VOCAL JAZZ (HIGH VOICE)
00843192 .... $16.99

132. STAN GETZ ESSENTIALS
00843193 .... $16.99

133. STAN GETZ FAVORITES
00843194 .... $16.99

134. NURSERY RHYMES*
00843196 .... $17.99

135. JEFF BECK
00843197 .... $16.99

136. NAT ADDERLEY
00843198 .... $16.99

137. WES MONTGOMERY
00843199 .... $16.99

138. FREDDIE HUBBARD
00843200 .... $16.99

139. JULIAN "CANNONBALL" ADDERLEY
00843201 .... $16.99

140. JOE ZAWINUL
00843202 .... $16.99

141. BILL EVANS STANDARDS
00843156 .... $16.99

142. CHARLIE PARKER GEMS
00843222 .... $16.99

143. JUST THE BLUES
00843223 .... $16.99

144. LEE MORGAN
00843229 .... $16.99

145. COUNTRY STANDARDS
00843230 .... $16.99

146. RAMSEY LEWIS
00843231 .... $16.99

147. SAMBA
00843232 .... $16.99

148. JOHN COLTRANE FAVORITES
00843233 .... $16.99

149. JOHN COLTRANE – GIANT STEPS
00843234 .... $16.99

150. JAZZ IMPROV BASICS
00843195 .... $19.99

151. MODERN JAZZ QUARTET CLASSICS
00843209 .... $16.99

152. J.J. JOHNSON
00843210 .... $16.99

153. KENNY GARRETT
00843212 .... $16.99

154. HENRY MANCINI
00843213 .... $16.99

155. SMOOTH JAZZ CLASSICS
00843215 .... $16.99

156. THELONIOUS MONK – EARLY GEMS
00843216 .... $16.99

157. HYMNS
00843217 .... $16.99

158. JAZZ COVERS ROCK
00843219 .... $16.99

159. MOZART
00843220 .... $16.99

160. GEORGE SHEARING
14041531 .... $16.99

161. DAVE BRUBECK
14041556 .... $16.99

162. BIG CHRISTMAS COLLECTION
00843221 .... $24.99

163. JOHN COLTRANE STANDARDS
00843235 .... $16.99

164. HERB ALPERT
14041775 .... $16.99

165. GEORGE BENSON
00843240 .... $16.99

166. ORNETTE COLEMAN
00843241 .... $16.99

167. JOHNNY MANDEL
00103642 .... $16.99

168. TADD DAMERON
00103663 .... $16.99

169. BEST JAZZ STANDARDS
00109249 .... $19.99

170. ULTIMATE JAZZ STANDARDS
00109250 .... $19.99

171. RADIOHEAD
00109305 .... $16.99

172. POP STANDARDS
00111669 .... $16.99

174. TIN PAN ALLEY
00119125 .... $16.99

175. TANGO
00119836 .... $16.99

176. JOHNNY MERCER
00119838 .... $16.99

177. THE II-V-I PROGRESSION
00843239 .... $19.99

178. JAZZ/FUNK
00121902 .... $16.99

179. MODAL JAZZ
00122273 .... $16.99

180. MICHAEL JACKSON
00122327 .... $16.99

181. BILLY JOEL
00122329 .... $16.99

182. "RHAPSODY IN BLUE" & 7 OTHER CLASSICAL-BASED JAZZ PIECES
00116847 .... $16.99

183. SONDHEIM
00126253 .... $16.99

184. JIMMY SMITH
00126943 .... $16.99

185. JAZZ FUSION
00127558 .... $16.99

186. JOE PASS
00128391 .... $16.99

187. CHRISTMAS FAVORITES
00128393 .... $16.99

188. PIAZZOLLA – 10 FAVORITE TUNES
48023253 .... $16.99

189. JOHN LENNON
00138678 .... $16.99

0418

*These do not include split tracks.